Decisions at 13/14+

Also by Michael Smith
and Veronica Matthew

Decisions at 15/16+

Decisions at 17/18+

Decisions at 13/14+

The starting point for GCSE options

Michael Smith
formerly Headmaster,
Filton High School, Bristol

Veronica Matthew
Senior Lecturer in Law
De Montfort University, Leicester

CRAC

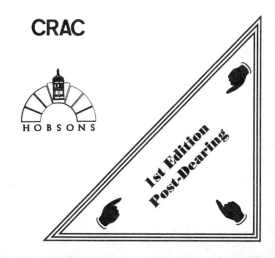

HOBSONS

1st Edition Post-Dearing

Acknowledgments

The authors wish to express their thanks to the following for their assistance:
Cornhill Insurance; all employers; examination groups; professional bodies; the Leicestershire Careers Service Information Unit, City Careers Centre, Pocklingtons Walk, Leicester, and regional councils for further education who have supplied information; John Laing, Kit Tyrell and Sue Smith. Peter Dines, sometime Deputy Chief Executive of the Secondary Examinations Council; and Principals of that Council for information on GCSE. The Controller of Her Majesty's Stationery Office; The Training Commission – Youth Training News; John Taylor and Tim Cornford of the National Curriculum Council; Paddy Radcliffe, Head of Careers at The Manor Community College, Cambridge; Louisa Prentis and her parents, and Mr F Murphy at The Manor Community College. The Director of Education, Avon County Council.

Note

Any reference to a person of one sex in this publication is to be taken as including a reference to the other sex, unless otherwise specified. No attempt has been made to give special consideration to Scottish school-leaving qualifications.

ISBN 1 85324 886 X

© 1976, 1980, 1983, 1985, 1988, 1993, 1994

Hobsons Publishing PLC, Bateman Street, Cambridge CB2 1LZ
First published 1972 by the Careers Research and
Advisory Centre
Second edition 1976, Hobsons Publishing PLC
Bateman Street, Cambridge CB2 1LZ
Reprinted 1977, 1978, 1979 (twice)
Third edition 1980, Hobsons Publishing PLC
Reprinted 1981, 1982 (twice)
Fourth edition 1983
Reprinted 1984 with new cover design and new series title
Decisions
Fifth edition 1985
Reprinted 1986
Sixth edition 1988
Reprinted 1989, 1990.
Revised 1993 with new cover design and new series title *Student Helpbooks*
Seventh edition 1994

CRAC

The Careers Research and Advisory Centre is a registered educational charity. Hobsons Publishing PLC produces CRAC publications under exclusive licence and royalty agreements.

Cover artwork by Amanda Hall
Text illustrations by Jon Riley
Printed and bound in Great Britain by Clays Ltd, St Ives plc, Bungay, Suffolk
Ref. L170/B/5/qq/C/JE

Contents
It's Your Choice

Introduction

These pages are intended for parents. They give a brief update on the changes to the curriculum at Key Stage 4.

Curriculum reform

During the latter part of 1993, there was mounting concern about the complexities and overprescription in the school curriculum for students aged 14–16 (Key Stage 4, or the GCSE years). The government asked Sir Ron Dearing, Chairman of the School Curriculum and Assessment Authority, to consult and reassess the situation, making recommendations for improvement. His report was published in January 1994 and accepted by the government.

Principal recommendations

In sum, he found that, without lessening the importance of English, maths and science as the basic core of the curriculum:

- greater flexibility should be allowed over subject choice for GCSE to ensure student motivation in these critical years
- the volume of subject material taught for GCSE should be reduced and programmes of study should be made clearer
- opportunity should be taken to introduce some vocational subjects that may involve assessment made by examining boards other than GCSE, but parallel in standard to them
- the 10-level scale to which you are becoming accustomed in assessing the development of your children should not be continued after the age of 14.

Why changes were necessary

Most teachers welcomed these changes because the National Curriculum was becoming too complicated. In addition, it was not allowing sufficient choice to meet the needs of children with particular abilities or disabilities. Differing, appropriate pathways are vitally important as children move towards adulthood. Throughout the report, it was stressed that GCSE should not be regarded as a terminus but merely a staging post on a learning process which stretches from 14 to 19. For the majority of students in the UK, 16 is no longer a preferred leaving age and should not be regarded as such.

Change and stability

It is always difficult to introduce changes into education while schooling is under way. Recognising this difficulty, the report ensures that:

- the changes do **not** affect those taking **GCSE examinations** in the summer of 1994 or 1995
- some **course** changes take effect for those **starting** GCSE courses in September 1994 leading to GCSE examinations in summer 1996
- other changes of **course** come into effect for those starting GCSE studies in September 1996
- **subject syllabuses and attainment targets** will also be reviewed for their content. It is therefore important to ensure that you have the correct up-to-date details of study programmes from the examination groups, when discussing them with your sons and daughters.

Every effort has been made in the text to point out the changes that will happen and the dates when they will occur.

1

It's Your Choice

Ready to Jump?

If you are over 13 and about to make your course choices for the next school year, this book is a MUST.

☛ Choosing your **options** can be a leap in the dark or a controlled jump where you know just where you are going.

☛ **GCSE** (General Certificate of Secondary Education) is ahead of you.

☛ **Career** requirements must be explored or you could miss out in the future.

This book aims to help you to get it right. You need to think your way through some rather important questions.

How are sensible decisions made?

What does it mean to study a particular subject?

What will be tested at the end of the course?

How will the testing be organised?

What do the GCSE grades mean?

How do GCSE grades match National Curriculum attainment targets?

Which subjects must I include?

Which subjects should I choose?

Which subjects should I leave out?

How do I make my choice?

These are vital questions. They all demand an answer. Get them wrong and you could find yourself in difficulties. Get them right and the two years from 14 to 16 could be the best springboard you ever landed on.

2 Making Decisions

This may be the first time you have been asked to make a decision which will affect your future. That may sound forbidding but you had better get used to the idea, for there are a whole series of them lurking around the corner.

D for Decision

Now   **The late 1990s and beyond**

These decisions are important for they will affect your life style which includes friends, holidays, bank balance, leisure interests and a whole range of satisfactions. They all connect.

Putting it this way makes it look automatic. But this is far from the case. The whole game is more like snakes and ladders. Above are the ladders – we've done away with the snakes. Take a look in the diary and see if you can find some.

Diary of a disaster about to happen

Extracts from David's diary

1994 January

Some great things about school this year. PE for a start. I'm in the Year 9 school soccer squad. There's a new teacher for science. Sue says he's horrible.

1994 March

Course choices for two years – that's donkey's years. I'm not looking forward to more science. Sue was right. Wish there was a GCSE in football. Old Smithy asked me today what I was doing for a career. How would I know? I think I'll just take single integrated science. I wonder what my mates are doing?

1996 August

Great week, GCSE results – 2Cs, 3Ds, 1F, 1G and a training place in Cooksons' Kitchens.

1997 July

Cooksons have offered me a permanent place in the kitchens. I was one of the lucky ones. Boss said I could be a manager if I took more exams. Wonder if I would pass them?

1997 August

Catering is OK. Better get on one of those advanced courses at the Tech. More qualifications mean more cash and that means better holidays. Just the job!

1997 Sept

Got a letter from Loamshire Tech. Did not have at least two grade Cs in double science, so they won't have me. Why don't they tell you these things? That's my promotion gone for a start.

1998 May

Can't get any further with this job. I'm stuck. Wonder if Mary's outfit has any jobs down the works. Careers Office might have something. If only I'd got things straight earlier.

Talking point

Can you spot the mistakes which David made between January 1994 and May 1998?

Five logical steps to making a decision

Below is a series of steps which, if you take them slowly, get your facts straight and take plenty of advice, should help you to come to a compromise solution. Remember you are not searching for *one* right answer. You are looking for one sensible answer among several.

1

Get the question clear.
What are you being asked?
What are the alternatives?
How important are they?

2

Find out the facts.
What do you need to know?
What are the facts?
Where can you obtain them?

3

Weigh them up.
Which facts matter most?
Which facts matter least?
Where do they lead?

4

Make the decision.
Which aspects come first?
What is the heart of the problem?
What follows?

5

Check results.
Does the decision look right?
Does the decision feel right?
When can changes come if needed?

Where shall we go for our holidays?

1 Get the question clear.
What do we all want from it?
Hotel or self-catering?
One place or moving around?
Inland or by the sea?

2 Find out the facts.
What do the travel firms offer?
How much do they charge?
What do the brochures say?
Who has been there and can tell us?

3 Weigh them up.
What are the important aspects?
What does not matter much?
Which is the most attractive?
Which has most to offer?

4 Make the decision.
When must it be made?
Have we thought of everything?
Can we afford it?
Is everyone happy with it?

5 Check results.
Did we enjoy the holiday?
Did it give all it promised?
Did we spend too much?
Would I recommend it?

Which subjects shall I choose?

Get the question clear.
What decisions have to be made?
Which subjects lead to exams?
How long have I to choose?
What's around to help me?

Find out the facts.
What subject skills do I need?
Are there new subjects?
What are my strengths?
What are my weaknesses?

Weigh them up.
What will I need for my career?
What if my career changes?
Is dropping subjects dangerous?
How can I get a balance?

Make the decision.
Has everyone been consulted?
Is this my own choice?
Am I happy with it?
Are there any doubts left over?

Check results.
Wait until the course starts.
Give each subject a fair trial.
Get advice if unhappy.
Don't leave it too long.

3 Why Must I Choose?

Fifty years ago there was no choice. The old School Certificate (the examination which existed even before O-levels) was just a pass/fail test with a set range of subjects. This may have been fine for the 1940s but it will not do for the 1990s and beyond to the twenty-first century. The world has moved on. The frontiers of knowledge have been pushed out. There is now more to know.

Some topics which could not have appeared in an examination course 50 years ago:

English	Writings of Boris Pasternak, John Osborne, Alan Sillitoe
Mathematics	Computer studies
History	The Cold War, conservation, carbon-dating
Geography	Nuclear power, North Sea gas, satellite weather forecasting
Biology	The electron microscope, structure of the cell, DNA
Chemistry	Polymer technology, radioactivity
Physics	The transistor, the microprocessor
Design studies	Plastics technology
Home economics	Microwave cookery
Music	The Beatles, Benjamin Britten
Drama	*The Caretaker, Guys and Dolls, Oliver*

To discover why there is choice, take a look at Fred – who is obviously in difficulties:

There are three problems lurking here

Time
Fred is trying to
beat the clock

Talents
with too much
on his plate

Choice
without it Fred
is unhappy

Translate this into Years 10 and 11 courses and the
reasons for choice become clear.

Time

Knowledge has extended to such a degree in so many
subjects that there is not enough time between now and
16 to study the whole range in sufficient depth. **So, we
choose.**

Talents

No one is good at everything, but each of us can be good
at something. If we study our best subjects in depth we
will improve our skills in them. **So, we choose**.

Choice

Personal likes and dislikes become more pronounced as
we grow older. By 14 our choices become more closely
linked to how well we get on with our subjects. **So, we
choose.**

4 **Getting a Balance**

Climbed any mountains lately?

One of the difficult aspects of preparing for outdoor pursuits is deciding what kit to take before starting out on an expedition. Too little will leave you unprepared for emergencies. Too much will weigh you down so that you can't cover the ground. If you expect one sort of weather condition you may be unprepared for another.

What will you take?

Tent with sewn-in groundsheets	Woollen shirts
Ropes	Spare clothes
Compass	Extra woollen socks
Bootlaces	Woollen trousers
Stretcher	Jeans
Whistles	Gloves
Radio	Water containers
Maps	Matches
Emergency rations	Sleeping bag
Crampons	Blankets
Skis	Sunglasses
Goggles	Flares
Dustbin liners	Climbing harnesses
Boots	Ice axe
Anorak	Splints
Sweaters	Torch
First-aid kit	Oxygen
Food	Alarm clock
Hurricane lamps	Plastic bags
Rucksack	Route cards
Thermal underwear	Waterproofs
Stoves and fuel	Suitcases
	Survival bags

You choose

The expedition is a two-day ascent in June of a 3,000-foot mountain. Ten miles are to be covered each day. Camp is at 1,200 feet. The weather forecast promises sun and rain. What gear would you take to achieve a balance of comfort, enjoyment and safety?

For the answer see page 150.

There is a curious feature in this kind of decision-making. Because you cannot accurately predict weather conditions, accidents, personalities, timing and gradients, you have to take a balanced range of resources to meet most known hazards. But when you come down the mountain and reach your base, you will know precisely what you should have taken.

There is a strong parallel with subjects available for GCSE.

Subject choice

English	French	Design and technology
Mathematics	German	
Physics	History	Religious education
Chemistry	Geography	
Biology	Business studies	Music
Single science	Art	Physical education
Double science	Food technology	

How do you know what you will need? Let us look at the situation.

Examine the things you know

1 You will – you hope – choose a career.
2 You know your strong subjects.
3 You know your weak subjects.
4 You know that results are important.
5 You know how well you work.
6 You know how you respond to a challenge.

Examine the things you do not know

1 You do not know which career it will be.
2 You cannot know the precise demands it will make.
3 You do not know how you or it will change.
4 You cannot predict changes in qualifications needed.
5 You cannot foresee your personal circumstances.
6 You do not know how technology may develop.

Choosing subjects against a range of knowns and unknowns is not easy. Just as in the mountain expedition, you need to ensure a

Each of the main subject areas will be useful to you at some time in the future. Think of each as a weight on a seesaw. Line up your weights so they balance.

What does each of these subject areas have to offer?

English

We cannot get far without words. They enable us to communicate. Most of the information we receive is passed on in words. When you have mastered the language you have a powerful tool at your disposal. The study of literature can be a most enriching experience. It should be an absolute essential for everyone.

Mathematics

More symbols. They enable us to make generalisations from exact data and are particularly helpful in solving real problems from models. They help us to recognise patterns and relationships and come to logical conclusions. This is not an area to fear. You probably know more mathematics than you think. Another 'must' for everybody.

Modern languages

When you can speak a foreign language you have an introduction to people whose speech, customs and culture are different from your own. International relationships have never been more important in economic, political and cultural terms. How can you sell anything to a country if you can't speak its language? From a career point of view, people who can speak another European language will be particularly useful. Most people believe this is another essential for all, now that Britain is a member of the European Community.

Science

Scientists ask questions and in order to find the answers, set up experiments and observe. The results, which are recorded accurately, help them to come to conclusions. You live in a technological world and without some scientific knowledge you will not be well enough equipped to understand it. So in one form or another, it is another 'must' for all.

Humanities

If you are curious about the world around you, about people and places, past and present, then these subjects (history, geography, religious education, etc) are for you. The skills and knowledge that you gain when you study the humanities will be very rewarding and many employers regard them highly when interviewing people for jobs.

Creative subjects

Whatever the medium–
drama, art or music–
creative work can be
intensely satisfying. To
explore form and space,
colour and sound,
material and matter,
involves a whole variety of
skills which are valuable
for both work and leisure.
They can also help you
earn your living – if you
are good at them.

Technological subjects

The application of scientific
ideas is at the core of good
design. Business, industry
and individual consumers
alike rely heavily on well-
designed, reliable technology.
No one whose working
career will span the twenty-
first century will be properly
equipped without a soundly
based experience of its
fundamentals.

What to aim for

In the end your choice will be a personal one – but wherever you are at school, whatever you are inclined towards and however many subjects you include, make absolutely sure that it is **balanced**.

> **English**
> **Mathematics**
> **A foreign language**
> **A science**
> **One of the humanities**
> **A creative subject**
> **A technological subject**

How the National Curriculum helps you to get this balance

The National Curriculum was first introduced into schools in 1989. This means that every state school run by a local education authority, or grant maintained school financed by central government, has to provide a basic curriculum consisting of religious education and subjects of the National Curriculum up to the end of Year 11.

To quote the law:

… schools must provide a balanced and broadly based curriculum which:
- ☞ promotes the spiritual, moral and cultural, mental and physical development of pupils at school and of society
- ☞ prepares pupils for the opportunities, responsibilities and experiences of adult life.

from the 1988 Education Act

Why have a National Curriculum?

The National Curriculum Council states that the National Curriculum will provide:

- ☞ **your teachers** with clear objectives for their teaching
- ☞ **you** with identifiable targets to aim for
- ☞ **your parents** with accurate information about what you can be expected to know, understand and be able to do
- ☞ **your future employers** with information about what you have actually achieved.

The overall result should mean that you have higher expectations and more effective progression throughout the years of full-time education, at the end of which you should be better prepared for life and work.

What subjects appear in the National Curriculum?

You will hear people refer to **core** and **foundation** subjects. All ten subjects which feature in the National Curriculum are foundation subjects, but three of them,

English

science

mathematics

are described as core subjects and were the first to be introduced. Up to the end of Key Stage 3 (ie up to the end of Year 9) the picture looked like this:

Core	Foundation
Mathematics	History
English	Geography
Science	Technology
Welsh*	Music
	Art
	A modern foreign language
	Physical education
	Welsh*

As well as religious education, the subjects above had to be taught.

* In Wales, Welsh will be a core subject in schools where it is the language every subject is taught in; in the remaining schools, it will be a foundation subject.

KEY STAGE 4 COURSE

As well as **religious education** (as an examination or non-
law, these are the **minimum** legal requirements for your patterr
the year in which you start.

60% of the study week	**KEY STAGE 4 STARTING 1993/4** CORE English Mathematics Science* (minimum, single science) [Welsh]+ FOUNDATION Modern foreign language ● (single subject or in combination) Information technology# Technology (single subject or in combination) OPTIONS	**KEY STAGE 4 STARTING 1994/5** CORE English Mathematics Science* (minimum, single science) [Welsh]+ FOUNDATION Modern foreign language ● (minimum ½ course except in Welsh schools) Physical education (not necessarily to GCSE) Technology should featur integrated approach or by subject. The situation OPTIONS
40% of the study week	Subjects here will vary from school to school. History, geograph prominently, so enabling you to select a balanced curriculum. Personal and social education, which will include careers educati	

ARRANGEMENTS 1993 – 1996

examination subject) which must form part of your studies by
of studies. You will see that there are differences according to

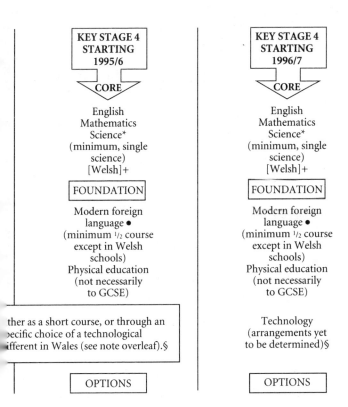

KEY STAGE 4 STARTING 1995/6	KEY STAGE 4 STARTING 1996/7
CORE	CORE
English Mathematics Science* (minimum, single science) [Welsh]+	English Mathematics Science* (minimum, single science) [Welsh]+
FOUNDATION	FOUNDATION
Modern foreign language ● (minimum ½ course except in Welsh schools) Physical education (not necessarily to GCSE)	Modern foreign language ● (minimum ½ course except in Welsh schools) Physical education (not necessarily to GCSE)
ther as a short course, or through an ecific choice of a technological ifferent in Wales (see note overleaf).§	Technology (arrangements yet to be determined)§
OPTIONS	OPTIONS

usic, art, drama, business studies and a second modern language will feature

Over the period of this table, an increasing number of
vocational subjects will be offered as options which will be assessed by non-GCSE
examination groups, but be equivalent in standard to them.

ken by everyone, will complete the picture.

* **Science** will more usually be offered as balanced science (an integration of physics, chemistry and biology). This can be studied as:

➻ single science 12.5% of the timetable
➻ double science 20% of the timetable
➻ double science will give you 2 GCSE awards.

The sciences can also be studied separately, but if all three are taken, some 30% of the week will be used up and this would upset your curriculum balance.

+ In Wales, **Welsh** will be a core subject only where it is the language in which all teaching takes place. In English-speaking schools in the Principality, it will be regarded as a second language and optional until 1999, when it will assume foundation status.

● It should be stressed that the **modern foreign language** requirement, allowable as a half course, represents a minimum. There is, as yet, no qualification available to measure it. You would be better advised to take a full GCSE course.

You will see that **information technology** appears as a separately assessed requirement in the 1993/4 column, but not subsequently. This is not because it ceases to be important. Rather, it is expected that skills in this mode of communication will be built in, as appropriate, to all subjects across the whole curriculum.

§ Because of its importance to the community, **technology** should continue to feature in courses starting in 1994 and 1995. However, the complexities of the 1993/4 arrangements have been lifted while planning is undertaken to redefine the subject for the start of the 1996/7 courses. The combined technology subjects offered by the examination groups in response to the

1993 requirement are, however, likely to be available in the short term.

In **Wales**, half courses in technology will not be offered and the subject will not be compulsory, though technology will continue to be offered as a GCSE option.

In **Wales**, modern foreign languages do not form part of the compulsory curriculum for students entering Key Stage 4 in September 1994. Half courses will not be available. Modern foreign languages form part of the options, either as a full GCSE or as a unit in a GNVQ course (see 'vocational qualifications', page 130).

Cross-curricular themes

Your school will also provide you with an education which meets the aims of the Education Reform Act with respect to preparing you for adult life and responsibilities. So, either directly linked to programmes of study and attainment targets or through personal and social education, you will have to consider:

- careers education and guidance
- health education
- citizenship
- environmental education
- economic and industrial understanding.

For an example of how these could apply, look at the chart which follows where each of them is related to a unit of work in **modern foreign languages**. But remember, they apply to all subjects.

Aspects of the five major cross-curricular themes are contained in the seven areas of experience. The table overleaf shows how a unit of MFL work might contribute to the themes, while reinforcing use of the target language.

CROSS-CURRICULAR THEMES

AREA OF EXPERIENCE: Everyday activities
MFL THEME: Home life

CROSS-CURRICULAR THEME	POSSIBLE FOCUS IN THE TARGET LANGUAGE
ECONOMIC AND INDUSTRIAL UNDERSTANDING	▷ eating out ▷ family spending and household budgets ▷ personal spending, eg. pocket money ▷ advertising
HEALTH EDUCATION	▷ personal hygiene routines, eg. cleaning teeth ▷ exercise routines ▷ getting on with others ▷ safety in the home
CAREERS EDUCATION AND GUIDANCE	▷ typical working day of employees in other countries ▷ who does what in the home and why
ENVIRONMENTAL EDUCATION	▷ forms of travel and their effects on the environment ▷ sources of noise pollution, eg. stereos, washing machines ▷ products used in the home, eg. environmentally friendly products, fast foods
EDUCATION FOR CITIZENSHIP	▷ leisure activities ▷ rules at home, punishments and rewards

Reproduced by permission of the National Curriculum Council

What about new subjects not offered before?

Many schools offer subjects in Years 10 and 11 that you will not have met before. These may make choice difficult but they often have important career significance.

Computer studies	This involves understanding logical thought processes, and the impact of computers and microprocessors on society.
Economics	This is a theoretically based subject, which studies the principles of money, trade, industry and financial processes.
Sociology	A people-based study concerned largely with groups of human beings and how they behave and interact with each other.
Keyboard skills	Basic skills which are very useful for those entering the secretarial world as well as for increasing personal competence in using computers for all careers.
Accounts/ business studies	An introductory course on commerce and financial control, providing another good insight into the business world.

Other options your school offers may include:

Art
Music
Drama
Classics (Latin or Greek)
Home economics/food technology
History/geography
The single/double science option
Various forms of design and technology
Second modern language.

There is nothing to stop you 'doubling up' on preferred curriculum areas, ie taking two modern foreign languages, doubling business studies or design and technology options.

5 Hurdles Ahead

This is the part you may think you won't like. First of all, however, cut exams down to size. They are not the most important part of the next two years. What you actually learn is far more valuable than any piece of paper which announces that you have a certificate in this or that. Certificates tell other people (employers or colleges) what subjects you have studied and the level you have reached in them. Think of exams as measuring instruments. You are not scared of scales or rulers, so you need not be frightened of exams if you have done your best over the past two years.

For some of you, public examinations will not be a new experience. Towards the end of Key Stage 3, many of you will have had your progress assessed by your teachers and you may also have taken Standard Attainment Tests (SATs) in mathematics, science and English. Taking your exams at the end of Key Stage 4 (at the end of Year 11) will just be an extension of this.

How testing is organised

In case you are not familiar with the new developments, let's map out the whole testing procedure from the age of 6 to 16. Particularly as you are coming in part way through, you need to appreciate the whole picture.

1 Targets

What are you aiming for in your studies?

Every subject you learn will have attainment **targets:**

- ⊷ **knowledge** – what you can remember
- ⊷ **understanding** – what you can explain
- ⊷ **skills** – what you can do.

Levels

How well did you achieve those targets?

These targets can be achieved at a variety of **levels** to which you were assessed up to Key Stage 3.

Knowledge	Understanding	Skills
A great deal ↕ Secure in simple facts	A thorough grasp ↕ Basic understanding	Very competent ↕ Can just cope

LEVELS
OF ACHIEVEMENT

The National Curriculum has 10 levels of achievement of the 10 curriculum subjects.

Children start working towards level 1 in each subject at the age of five. Different children will move up the levels at different speeds, but most are likely to move on by one level every two years.

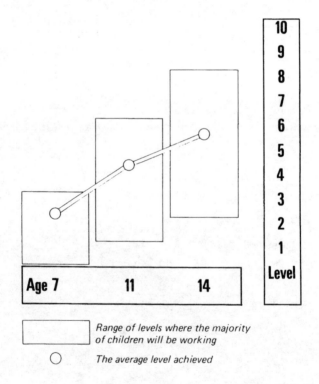

Range of levels where the majority of children will be working

The average level achieved

3 Milestones

When are these achievements measured?

Milestones along the way are now called **Key Stages**. Had your time in school so far been in the shadow of the National Curriculum, you would have passed through two stages before entering secondary school and you arc now completing **Key Stage 3**.

Up to now students have been assessed at the end of each Key Stage. The diagram on the next page shows how your age relates to the milestones.

The levels you can achieve are numbered 1 – 10. The graph on the previous page shows how and when these levels could be secured – especially as you pass through **Key Stage 3**.

In **Key Stage 4**, however, you will be assessed by GCSE grades.

ASSESSMENT

Pupil progress is monitored continuously by teachers, but formal assessment takes place at the ages of 7, 11, 14 and 16. These ages mark the end of the four key stages which cover the 11 years of compulsory education.

AGES

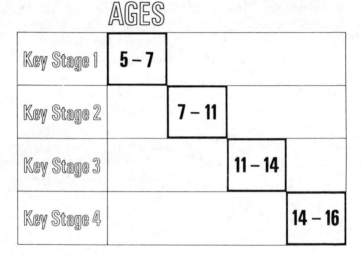

Key Stage 1	**5 – 7**			
Key Stage 2		**7 – 11**		
Key Stage 3			**11 – 14**	
Key Stage 4				**14 – 16**

National Curriculum assessment is not a pass/fail system. It gives teachers the feedback they need to plan teaching at the right level for individual pupils; helps to identify learning difficulties; and provides information for parents and others.

The systematic record-keeping made possible by assessment helps to ensure progression, so that a different teacher or school can build on what the pupil has already achieved.

How does all this relate to GCSE?

For those taking GCSE, there are seven grades which are passes and an ungraded category which is a fail.

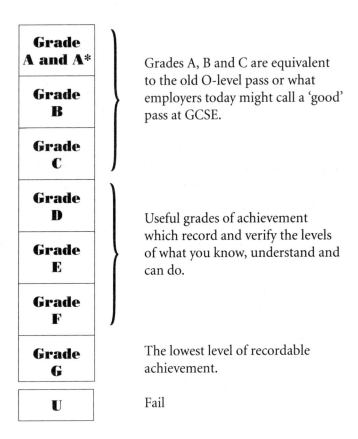

Grade A and A*	Grades A, B and C are equivalent to the old O-level pass or what employers today might call a 'good' pass at GCSE.
Grade B	
Grade C	
Grade D	Useful grades of achievement which record and verify the levels of what you know, understand and can do.
Grade E	
Grade F	
Grade G	The lowest level of recordable achievement.
U	Fail

In the future it may be that these grades will be progressively lined up with a National Curriculum extended scale of attainment targets from level 4 to level 10, but not yet.

From September 1994 there will be a 'super A' grade, to be known as A starred. This will be awarded to students who have performed outstandingly well at the A grade level.

What does this mean for your timetabled subjects?

All this means a much sharper focus for learning. What you are expected to know, understand and be good at can be **translated** into subject **theories** and **skills**. This should help you know where you are and where you are going – valuable pointers to help you eventually get there!

The attainment targets for

> **English**
>
> **Mathematics**
>
> **Science**
>
> **Modern foreign languages**

have been fully worked out for Key Stage 4 though may be subject to amendment during the coming months.

SUBJECT ATTAINMENT TARGETS

Attainment targets define the knowledge, skills and understanding pupils are expected to have by the end of each key stage. Each of the attainment targets is defined further through statements of attainment spread over 10 levels of difficulty.

SUBJECT	ATTAINMENT TARGETS
ENGLISH	Speaking and listening; reading; writing; spelling; handwriting.
MATHEMATICS	Using and applying mathematics; number; algebra; shape and space; handling data.
SCIENCE	Scientific investigation; life and living processes; materials and their properties; physical processes.
TECHNOLOGY	Identifying needs and opportunities; generating a design; planning and making; evaluating; information technology capability.
HISTORY	Knowledge and understanding of history; interpretations of history; the use of historical sources.
GEOGRAPHY	Geographical skills; knowledge and understanding of places; physical geography; human geography; environmental geography.
MODERN FOREIGN LANGUAGES	Listening; speaking; reading; writing.
ART	Investigating and making; knowledge and understanding.
MUSIC	Performing and composing; listening and appraising.
PHYSICAL EDUCATION	End of key stage statements and programme of study (general), programmes of study (specific activity).

☞ Now let's take ☞

☞ a longer look at ☞

☞ GCSE ☞

☞ at present ☞

The General Certificate of Secondary Education

The important things about GCSE are as follows:

☞ It is a single-subject exam. You can sit as few or as many subjects as you like. Those in which you achieve a grade will appear on your certificate.

☞ The normal age for sitting it will be 16+, at the end of Year 11. You can, however, take it earlier or later or more than once if your school advises.

☞ GCSE is run by:

Six examining groups

The University of London Examinations and Assessment Council (ULEAC)

The Midland Examining Group (MEG)

The Northern Examining and Assessment Board (NEAB)

The Northern Ireland Schools Examination Council (NISEC)

The Southern Examining Group (SEG)

The Welsh Joint Education Committee (WJEC)

☛ Schools are free to choose their groups, so you could sit exams run by different groups. There will, however, be a common timetable operating over all.
☛ Certificates will be awarded on a single scale of seven grades.
☛ The exam is open to anyone.

Making examinations fair

How does anyone know that a grade C in English achieved in Berwick-on-Tweed is equivalent to a grade C in English taken in Bristol? What are the guarantees? How are they ensured? It would be unfair if one were easier than the other.

To ensure fairness and equality, GCSE has certain safeguards which apply to the exam as a whole and to individual subjects. These safeguards will apply whichever group's exams you sit. They are

national specifications for all exams

All the exams are designed to measure what you

Know
Understand
Can do

There will often be papers representing different levels of difficulty so that your knowledge, understanding and ability can be properly tested and you can be awarded a grade which fairly states just how good you are at a subject.

Guarantees operating within subjects

These guarantees must be honoured by all the examining groups offering a particular subject. They require the group to:

- ☞ set out a clear title and make sure that the subject content does not overlap with any other

- ☞ explain clearly the aim of the course

- ☞ offer you enough experiences during the course to enable you to achieve any of the seven grades

- ☞ avoid making unreasonable demands on you

- ☞ try not to be too expensive

- ☞ provide opportunities for both your own teacher and an external examiner to have a say in your final result

- ☞ make the assessment objectives clear

- ☞ help you relate the course to life

- ☞ explain clearly exactly what can be expected from anyone who achieves them.

How you will be awarded your grades

The seven GCSE grades cover an enormous range of talent – from the very good indeed to the reasonably competent. Examiners could measure this in a variety of ways.

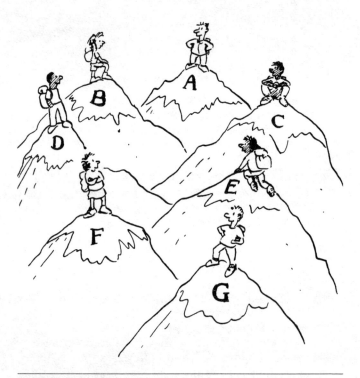

For example

1 Papers of increasing difficulty

The exam could be organised in a series of papers, or questions within papers, which get increasingly difficult.

or

There could be broad questions which everyone can answer but which have more demanding parts to them.

2 Common and optional papers

The exam could be organised in three papers. Everyone would take paper 2, after which candidates could choose between a more difficult paper 3 or an easier paper 1.

3 Grade-related papers

Under this system the papers you took would lead to a range of grades. For example:

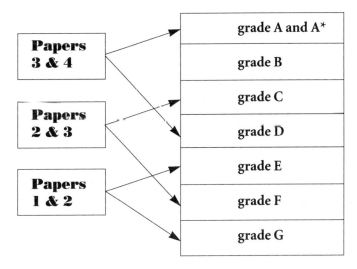

If you sat papers 1 and 2 only, your final result could only lie between grades E and G. It would not be possible to achieve a grade higher than E. To get higher grades you would have to take papers 2 and 3 which lead to a grade between C and F. In order to obtain a grade A you would have to take papers 3 and 4.

Your subject teacher will make clear to you how the GCSE papers you will sit are designed.

What about coursework?

Everybody has heard about coursework! Rumours are rife and some people think they will be struck down by it like a disease, so let's get it into perspective. There are some basic points to be clear about.

☞ Every subject has some form of compulsory coursework.

☞ Coursework is important because it assesses what you can do outside a two-hour paper in an examination room – like managing a long-term investigation or playing in a musical group. It's all about what you can research on a topic and gives you an opportunity to show up well.

☞ It is important because at least 20% of the final result comes from the coursework mark. In many subjects it will be higher (see page 51).

☞ The principal difficulty is one of organisation, and there will be some time-juggling to do. You may have several pieces of coursework on the go at the same time, being worked on partly at home and partly at school. If you feel snowed under, your first move is to talk it over with the appropriate subject teacher who will help you sort it out.

☛ Coursework does not suit the 'let's put it off until tomorrow' person. If you continually do this, you will not survive. Get down to it sensibly; think, plan and organise carefully and you will experience a great sense of achievement.

☛ Coursework can also be carried over into the sixth form and offered again in a retake of a GCSE exam.

☛ Spelling is now an important aspect which is tested in all subjects at GCSE. Five per cent of the marks are reserved for correct spelling in all subjects. This applies to both coursework and examination papers.

Coursework limits* for Key Stage 4

Course beginning	Subject	Coursework limits
September 1992	English	40%†
	English literature	30%
	Mathematics	20%
	Science	30%

† Up to 20% for Attainment Target 1 (Speaking and Listening) and up to 20% between Attainment Targets 2 and 3 (Reading and Writing).

September 1993	Biology	30%
	Chemistry	30%
	Physics	30%
	Technology	60%
September 1994	Geography	25%
	History	25%
September 1995	Modern foreign languages (provisional)	30%

* NB Some examining groups may set lower limits for coursework in particular syllabuses.

How many examination subjects should I take?

It is difficult to generalise. Each person is different. If you are taking subjects which, at the time you are sitting the examination, are formally part of the National Curriculum foundation subjects, you will be required to have your abilities tested and examinations in these subjects will normally be compulsory.

As far as subjects outside the National Curriculum are concerned, take as many as you can without overstretching yourself. As you may not achieve all the grades you hope for, it is a good idea to take more subjects than you need, but don't go to extremes. It is better to obtain six GCSEs with good grades than ten GCSEs with low grades.

6 What Am I in For?

There is nothing like knowing where you are going! The broad journey plan suggesting a balance was set out on page 17, but you are now going to have to decide which subjects you will take in order to implement the plan. One way of choosing is to look at the aims of a course and the kind of examination that concludes it.

The national specifications and guidelines mentioned earlier set out exactly what a course is like and what the examiners are looking for.

In this chapter you will find:

☞ brief summaries of the course aims
☞ assessment objectives
☞ an indication of the form of the examination.

There is also another way to look at your future. You could use **skills** as the starting point. On pages 92 and 93 you will see a table of skills which shows you the subjects in which they can be best developed.

Important

In the pages which follow you must not assume that every aspect of the subject course and assessment objective is listed.

Here are only summaries, intended to convey a flavour of the programmes of study and assessment techniques ahead of you.

To find out more:

1. List the subjects in which you are particularly interested.
2. Find out from your school which examination group's syllabus and exam is used.
3. Consult the full prospectus published by the group.
4. Become familiar with the attainment targets published by the School Curriculum and Assessment Authority.

Art and design

The **course** is about expressing ideas with hand and eye and providing you with the opportunity of presenting your ideas, imagination and feelings creatively. If you choose this subject, your visual awareness should sharpen, your practical artistic skills develop and your self-confidence increase. You will be able to follow a broad course in art and design or specialise in one of the subject areas: drawing and painting; graphics; textiles; three-dimensional studies; photography.

In exploring elements like line, shape, form, colour, tone, pattern and texture, you would be expected to:

☞ respond creatively to an idea, theme or subject
☞ record from direct observation or personal experience
☞ pursue a design from the idea stage to practical completion
☞ work on your own
☞ analyse ideas, and to research and communicate them
☞ blend materials, ideas and techniques sympathetically
☞ choose and use materials economically
☞ use and compose line, tone, colour, pattern, texture, shape, form and space.

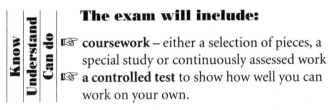

Know Understand Can do

The exam will include:

☞ **coursework** – either a selection of pieces, a special study or continuously assessed work
☞ **a controlled test** to show how well you can work on your own.

Art is a subject which relies heavily on developing skills for success, from Key Stage 1 to Key Stage 4. At all stages you should be making clear connections with artists who have made an important cultural contribution. The diagram on the next page shows this for Key Stages 1 – 3 and you should expect this to continue throughout Key Stage 4.

SUBJECT KNOWLEDGE: ART

Pupils need a developing grasp of 'what counts as art'. They need to look at, among other things:

O art from different cultures and times;

O pottery, weaving, clothing, buildings;

O posters, sculptures and paintings;

O television commercials;

O portraits;

O prints.

It is important that connections are made both to pupils' own work and to the connections between artists (AT2, strand 2)

Pupils' practical work	Connections	Key Stage
Drawing and painting flowers	William Morris, van Gogh, Georgia O'Keeffe	1
Experimenting with colours to represent 'sky'	Claude, Constable, Hiroshige	2
Using discarded objects to construct a new design	Picasso's use of a bicycle seat as the head of a bull; Miro	3
Experimenting with materials — clay, plaster, wire	Hepworth, Epstein, Giacometti, Cornell, Gabo, Schwitters	3
Painting trees in blossom	Palmer, Monet, the Indian and Persian miniaturists	2
Landscapes	Turner, Constable, Japanese wood blocks	3

Business studies

The aims of the **course** are that you should:

☞ know about the business world and how it works
☞ understand the way that major organisations affect business
☞ appreciate how competition and monopoly work
☞ explore the way in which commercial enterprises are organised, are financed and work together
☞ understand the way that economics affect business activity
☞ find out how the business world affects society, both in theory and from your own practical experience
☞ become aware of business language
☞ be able to select, handle and present information and data effectively
☞ become aware of the importance of change.

In the exam you will be expected to:

Know
Understand
Can do

☞ demonstrate your knowledge of the business world
☞ express ideas in words, figures and graphs
☞ show your understanding of business figures and themes
☞ choose, interpret and apply facts and figures
☞ solve business problems
☞ distinguish between evidence and opinion.

The exam will comprise:

Know	Understand	Can do

☞ **written papers** with particular emphasis on questions which present you with facts to work on

☞ possibly an **oral examination**

☞ **compulsory coursework** (which is likely to be about 25% of the total marks); it could be in the form of continuous assessment or a number of special assignments.

Classical subjects

This is an umbrella title which covers the Latin and Greek civilisations and their people's languages. It relates to language courses (indicated L below) and non-language courses (indicated NL below). The schemes are complex and interested students are strongly advised to consult the full syllabus.

The **courses** should enable you to:

☞ develop a competence in one of the languages (L)

☞ read, understand and appreciate some literature in the original (L) or in translation (NL), and respond to it (L and NL)

☞ understand the civilisation (L), paying particular attention to the art, literary and archaeological evidence (NL)

☞ appreciate the relationship of a classical language to English (L and NL)

☞ observe and analyse information critically (L and NL).

In the exam you will be expected to:

☞ **Language**

- demonstrate your language ability
- show understanding of prepared texts in at least two of poetry, prose and drama
- answer questions on literature, life, history and customs of Greece or Rome (between 10 and 25%).

☞ **Non-language**

- answer multiple-choice or stimulus questions to demonstrate your knowledge of the classical world
- answer questions on literature in translation and show how evidence is used.

(margin: Know — Understand — Can do)

In the non-language course, assessed coursework will be required and will account for 20–25% of the marks.

Design and technology

The requirements for 1993/4 for design and technology were complicated and not all the possibilities listed here were on offer at your school. They are explained here because some of the GCSE design and technology subjects now on offer came from them. Everyone in that year had to include design and technology amongst the group of foundation subjects. There were variations, however.

☞ All subjects had to include programmes of study to meet attainment targets.

Te 1 Identifying needs and opportunities

Te 2 Generalising ideas

Te 3 Planning and working

Te 4 Evaluating

☞ Information technology (attainment target Te 5) could be studied separately or as part of a design and technology course.

☞ Full courses in technology and in design and technology required students to work with one other material, eg food, graphic media or textiles.

☞ You could study your design and technology (D&T) as a full or short course, but if you chose the latter your information technology (IT) had to be separately asssessed.

For Key Stage 4 studies in 1993/4

Setting this out in terms of **syllabuses** (or programmes of study), the possibilities were as follows.

Technology
You could work towards attainment targets Te 1– Te 4, using construction materials together with units from food, graphic media or textiles. IT would be an integral component.

Technology and a related subject
This could be a short course in technology in combination with an allied field of study, eg electronics or catering. All attainment targets would be assessed.

Design and technology
D&T could be a full course but restricting assessment to attainment targets Te 1–Te 4. There could be components from other technological areas, but information technology would be assessed separately.

Information technology
This could be a programme of study to enable students to be assessed for Te 5. It could be in relation to another subject to which it has application.

This is how the variations for Key Stage 4 studies in **1993/4** looked.

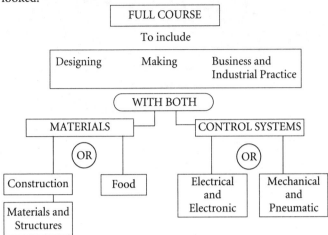

You would have undertaken two designing and making tasks, one of which would have been a substantial project set in a broad vocational context, such as manufacturing, construction and engineering.

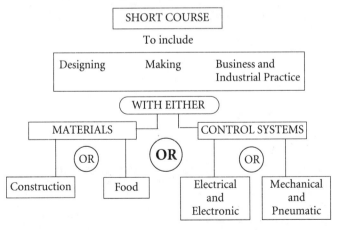

You would have undertaken one designing and making task, which would have been within a broad vocational context such as manufacturing, construction or engineering.

Design and technology courses likely for 1994/5

As well as the usual design and technology subjects the **combined subject** technology GCSE syllabuses are many and varied. Each one leads to a single GCSE award in the combined subject concerned.

Technology and a related subject

☞ art
building studies
catering
economics
electronics
fashion
music

Design and technology and a related subject

☞ art
automation
building studies
the built environment
business studies
catering
drama
economics
electronics
fashion
music
product design

Information technology and a related subject

☞ art
building studies
business studies
catering
economics
electronics
fashion

Some restrictions

There are some restrictions that prevent anyone from working on two GCSE syllabuses which have considerable subject overlap.

It would not be possible for you to study:

☞ GCSE technology with GCSE design and technology
☞ GCSE technology with GCSE information systems
☞ GCSE technology with GCSE technology and art (combined)
☞ GCSE D&T and catering (combined) with GCSE D&T and fashion (combined)
☞ GCSE D&T and electronics (combined) with GCSE electronics.

The common aims of all these types of course are to:

☞ describe and apply the principles/ideas of design to manufactured articles
☞ show which problems can be solved by practical or technological means
☞ enable you to design articles which look good, work and are cost effective
☞ evaluate finished products
☞ make sure good safety practices have been observed.

The exams of all the courses will test your:

☞ design skills
☞ making and assembling skills
☞ knowledge of principles
☞ ability to communicate.

The exams will include:

☞ **open-ended written questions**
☞ perhaps an **oral test**
☞ **solving** design problems
☞ **making** articles
☞ **coursework** – accounting for up to 60% of your marks.

Know Understand Can do

Your personal folio of work, which could include mock-ups of models, will be important.

Economics

The aim of the **course** is to help you to understand how the world's scarce resources might best be used. You will learn how the British economy works and how it affects individuals, groups and organisations. You will pick up the language and terms economists use and get some practice in handling facts and figures. The ability to distinguish between evidence and opinion will be important. At the end of the course you should be in a better position to make informed decisions, both as a consumer and a producer.

In the exam you will be expected to:

☞ recall and understand the principal facts which lie behind the way the economy works

☞ use this knowledge in words, calculations, graphs and pictures

☞ show you can use the appropriate terms properly

☞ choose, analyse, interpret and apply facts and figures

☞ distinguish between evidence and opinion, making sensible judgments and expressing them.

The exam will consist of:

☞ **question papers** containing a variety of approaches – short answers, multiple choice, structured essays or continuous writing

☞ **coursework** assessed by your teachers, carrying 25% of the marks.

(side tab, rotated) **Know Understand Can do**

Science

The aims of the **course** set out below are consistent with the requirements of the National Curriculum Order for science and describe the educational purposes of a National Curriculum course for the GCSE examination in science: double award or science: single award.

1 To provide, through the exploration and study of science, a coherent educational experience which enables you to acquire sufficient understanding and knowledge to:

☞ become confident citizens in a technological world, able to take or develop an informed interest in matters of scientific importance

☞ recognise the usefulness and limitations of scientific methods and appreciate their applicability in other disciplines and in everyday life

☞ be encouraged to pursue and be suitably prepared for further studies in science.

2 To develop abilities and skills that:

☞ are relevant to the study, practice and application of science

☞ are useful in everyday life

☞ encourage safe practice.

3 To stimulate:

☞ curiosity, interest and enjoyment in science and its methods of enquiry

☞ an interest in, and care for, the environment.

4 To promote awareness that:

☞ the study and practice of science are co-operative and cumulative activities and are subject to social, economic, technological, ethical and cultural influences and limitations

☞ the application of science may be both beneficial and detrimental to the individual, the community and the environment

☞ the concepts of science are of a developing and sometimes temporary nature.

Different examining groups will arrange their programmes of study in different ways. There follows an example from the Midland Examining Group. This syllabus covers 18 topics to be studied over two years.

Syllabus

1	Sound & hearing	11	Energy flow & ecosystems
2	Light & sight	12	Weather & atmosphere
3	Space & communication	13	Rocks
4	Feedback & control	14	Plants
5	Raw materials	15	Animals
6	Reactions	16	The body at work
7	Structures & properties	17	Plants at work
8	Patterns & trends	18	Forces & machines
9	Electricity & magnetism		
10	Fuels & energy sources		

Assessment objectives

For full details, consult the National Curriculum statement of attainment targets, but in summary they highlight:

Know | Understand | Can do

☞ **scientific investigation** – how good you are at:
- asking questions, making predictions and developing theories
- observing, measuring and handling variable factors
- interpreting results and evaluating scientific evidence.

☞ **knowing and understanding science**
- an appreciation of life and living processes
- a knowledge and understanding of materials and their properties as well as physical processes
- the ability to communicate scientific observations, select data, interpret it and make deductions
- the ability to use science to solve problems.

The exam is designed to cater for different levels of ability and you will find that different papers lead to different National Curriculum attainment levels.

Tier	Description	Levels available	Duration
1	Written paper 1 Written paper 2	3 – 6 3 – 6	1hr 15min 1hr 15min
2	Written paper 3 Written paper 4	5 – 8 5 – 8	1hr 45min 1hr 45min
3	Written paper 5 Written paper 6	7 – 10 7 – 10	2hr 2hr

Example from the Midland Examining Group

75% of the GCSE grade is provided from written examination and 25% from coursework. You will be entered for the tier most appropriate to your progress.

Single or double?

This will be a matter of personal preference but you should be aware of certain career limitations if only single balanced science is chosen.

Science is not in a vacuum

You should never see any of your subjects in isolation one from another. Science is a good example where:

☞ important connections are made across the curriculum with other **subjects**

☞ **skills** are developed which, in themselves, are not only related to science

☞ **themes** are involved which go well beyond the subject areas which science normally covers

☞ **dimensions** common to every subject are explored.

To make this clear, look at the spidery network opposite.

SCIENCE LINKS

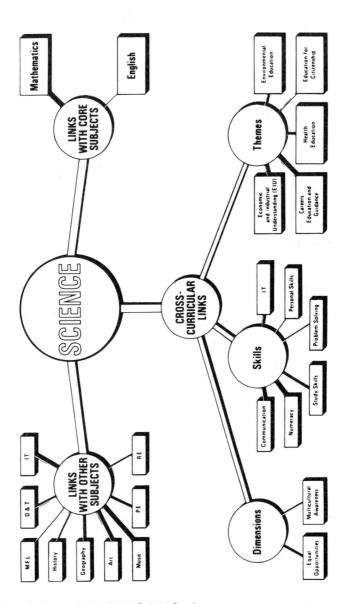

Names

You may find science courses referred to as balanced, integrated, modular or separate. Each has a different emphasis:

☞ **balanced** – where separate areas are clear, but all three science strands are studied in conjunction with each other
☞ **integrated** – where theories are arranged to stress inter-relationships and particular ideas
☞ **modular** –where theories are organised into separate units of teaching and assessment
☞ **separate** – where physics, chemistry and biology are taught independently of each other.

English

The aims of the **English course** are that you should:

☞ understand facts, ideas and opinions as you pass on information
☞ be critical of what you read and be able to sort out ideas for particular purposes
☞ be able to talk about experiences
☞ know how the English language is structured
☞ be able to use spoken English
☞ be aware of the differences between formal and informal English.

There are three **attainment targets**. They are:

☞ **speaking and listening,** in which you will have the chance to show how well you can:

- – put experience into words, expressing what you feel and imagine
- – understand, order and present facts, ideas and opinions
- – show a sense of audience and an awareness of style in a variety of situations
- – recognise different levels and kinds of meaning in a variety of contexts
- – make a personal response to what you hear, read and understand
- – reflect on the way other people communicate.

☞ **reading**, in which you will be able to show that you can:

- – get hold of facts, ideas and opinions
- – recognise different sorts of meanings
- – understand how writers use language to get the effects they want.

☞ **writing** in which you will have plenty of opportunity to show that you can:

- – write about personal feelings
- – understand and present facts, ideas and opinions
- – show you can appreciate good grammar by using it well
- – understand how flexible a tool language is to express what you want to say.

Correct spelling, good handwriting and careful presentation will all be important here!

Coursework could count for up to 40% of the marks (see page 51).

Your assessment

There will be coursework and a final examination which can be sat in three tiers (or expected levels of outcome). You can only sit for one tier. They are arranged in this kind of pattern.

Level awarded (target levels ringed)

Tier 1	④	⑤	6			
Tier 2		5	⑥	⑦	⑧	⑨	10
Tier 3				7	⑧	⑨	⑩

Example from WJEC

Details will, however, vary between examination groups.

English literature

This is a separate examination but it follows the same
pattern as English language.

In particular, **you would be expected to:**

☞ get to know the literature well
☞ understand the themes beneath the surface
☞ recognise the ways that writers achieve their effects
☞ understand the way human characteristics are
   portrayed
☞ make a personal and informed response to the
   literature being studied.

Drama

Your school may offer drama (sometimes called theatre
studies) as one of its creative arts options. It is an
important and exciting option, but you need to be clear
about its intentions. The course is NOT there to produce
actors or stage technicians.

In the world of work employers are seeking people with well-developed personal qualities. Employers want people who:

☞ can solve problems
☞ can think on their feet
☞ are totally reliable
☞ can work in teams
☞ can communicate well.

Drama provides all these skills. All theatre productions you have ever seen are good only if those skills are highly developed on and behind the stage. In addition, success in a subject like this can give you plenty of personal satisfaction and a lifelong leisure interest.

In the **course** you would be working on prepared pieces – performances based on a variety of texts as well as self-devised pieces where, as a team, you would be writing and acting a script for a specific audience – like producing a play on the theme of 'change' for junior schools. You would be learning about acting, design and technical support; be introduced to improvisation and scriptwriting, as well as studying text interpretation. Opportunities are likely to be taken to visit theatres frequently.

For the exam, the assessment is a practical business and you would be tested on your ability to:

Know Understand Can do

☞ understand how a piece of drama is devised
☞ demonstrate technique
☞ organise a performance
☞ interpret a script
☞ be aware of the contribution of design and technology
☞ appreciate performances of others
☞ explore social and personal issues through the medium of drama.

Geography

The aim of the **geography course** is to give you an understanding of the nature of the Earth's surface, the character of places and how human beings interact with their environment. Your studies will include enquiries on small, regional, national and international scales. Overall, the course should enable you to make more sense of the world and encourage you to hold informed views on rapidly changing world issues.

In the exam you will be expected to:

☞ show an awareness of places in relation to others

☞ explain your understanding of environments and the processes which affect them (economic and technological developments)

☞ show that you understand how people interact with their environment

☞ be aware of communities and cultures both in our society and elsewhere

☞ demonstrate a range of skills developed through practical work: observing, fact-finding and analysis, using books, maps and photographs

☞ show sensitivity to the environment and an awareness of the contrasts between rich and poor nations.

Know   Understand   Can do

The exam will include:

Know | Understand | Can do

☞ one or more **question papers** containing a variety of stimulus questions – maps, photographs and statistics to analyse and comment on

☞ **fieldwork, coursework** and **regular assignments** – assessed by your teachers, and accounting for at least 20% (but not more than 25%) of the overall final mark.

History

The **history course** will bring the past alive. It will encourage you to develop an enthusiasm for using the evidence to discover what it was like to live in a different time from your own, and to make comparisons. Whatever period of history you study, you will explore cause and consequence, continuity and change, similarity and difference. The development of particular skills will be important: how to find out information from first-hand sources and from other people's writings, how to spot bias, how to present what you have discovered in a logical way. Hopefully you will develop an interest in history which will continue long after you leave school.

Know | Understand | Can do

In the exam you will be expected to:

☞ recall and select knowledge, setting it out clearly

☞ show that you understand something of the pattern of historical development

Know | Understand | Can do

☞ prove you can explore history using a variety of sources – evidence of the time, objects, books, statistics and word of mouth

☞ interpret your findings, sorting out fact from opinion and detecting bias

☞ reach balanced conclusions.

The exam will include:

☞ **questions** which will ask you to respond to a variety of forms of historical evidence

☞ **short-answer questions** to test knowledge and understanding

☞ **questions** which require you to write continuous prose, but not necessarily long essays

☞ **coursework** assessed by your teachers, accounting for at least 20% of your marks (but not more that 25%).

Home economics

The **course** in home economics explores the physical, social, economic and design needs of the home in general, and food, clothing and shelter in particular. It helps you, as a future homemaker, to improve your skills in managing resources and helps you to become an effective member of a family, the community and society. Both theory and practice are seen as important and there will be emphasis on problem-solving and decision-making. Home economics covers the home, family, food and textiles and the application of human skill, effort, money, time and materials to them. You will be expected to investigate, analyse, interpret and discriminate before turning theory into practice. After covering this common background, you will be able to specialise in one aspect of the home: family, food or textiles.

In the exam you will be expected to:

☞ appreciate how aspects of homemaking work together

☞ explain human needs at various stages of life

☞ know how a family works as an effective unit

☞ prove you have the skills to meet short-term needs and to appreciate long-term needs

☞ be aware of technological changes and how they affect the home

☞ display a critical awareness of advertising

☞ know the requirements of good safety practices.

The exam will include:

☞ a variety of written and practical tests.

Know Understand Can do

Mathematics

The **mathematics course** aims to increase your confidence by improving your skills in oral, written and practical maths. It endeavours to give you a feel for

numbers and to enable you to understand the meaning of the results you get. Problem-solving, presentation and result-checking are important, as is coming to grips with mathematical principles. The broader aspects of maths will not be ignored – applying maths to everyday situations and understanding the part it plays in the world around you. You will be expected to recognise when new situations can best be represented mathematically and to decide which methods are best suited to solve problems. The relationship between maths, science and technology will be made clear, as will the patterns and relationships within the subject itself. Individual enquiry and experiment will be important as you develop the ability to reason logically, classify, generalise and prove. Essentially, maths is communication.

Know | Understand | Can do

In the exam you will be expected to:

- ☞ recall, use and apply maths in many situations using your problem-solving skills clearly and logically
- ☞ use tables, graphs and diagrams
- ☞ understand measurement using appropriate instruments (including calculators) accurately
- ☞ recognise and express patterns in maths
- ☞ carry out practical work on an extended basis.

The exam will not include a common paper to suit all grades. You will take an end-of-course paper appropriate to your ability.

- ☞ **Coursework** will account for 20% of the marks.

Attainment targets

There are five of these, each one containing three or four strands.

Attainment targets	Strands
1 Using and applying mathematics	Applications Mathematical communication Reasoning, logic and proof
2 Number	Knowledge and use of numbers Estimation and approximation Measures
3 Algebra	Patterns and relationships Formulae, equations and inequalities Graphical representation
4 Shape and space	Shape Location Movement Measures
5 Handling data	Collecting and processing Representing and interpreting Probability

Levels of assessment

The exams themselves are arranged on a three-tier basis, very similar to the pattern for English and science. An example from the Southern Examining Group follows.

Levels awarded (target levels ringed)

Foundation   ③ ④ ⑤ ⑥ 7

Intermediate   4 ⑤ ⑥ ⑦ ⑧ 9

Higher   6 ⑦ ⑧ ⑨ ⑩

Great care should be taken in selecting the level of examination taken. A weak candidate choosing the higher level papers just failing to achieve level 7 would not get a 6, but an ungraded result.

Modern foreign languages

You have only to spend a holiday outside the United Kingdom in continental Europe to be aware of the importance of a modern foreign language. You can't go far without some skill in it if you are going to appreciate what is going on around you and make yourself understood.

But it's not just a matter of speaking to understand and be understood. A study of MFL (as they are increasingly called) will introduce you to the culture and civilisation of the country and help you appreciate it better. Using the target language chosen is intended to be both enjoyable and intellectually stimulating, not just between you and your teacher in school but beyond the classroom to the world outside for the rest of your life.

Your confidence and experience is built up each time you have an MFL lesson.

Know Understand Can do

In the exam you will be expected to show some ability in

☞ **listening** – understanding announcements, requests and conversations

☞ **reading** – understanding public notices and signs like menus, timetables and brochures

Know Understand Can do

☞ **speaking** – responding to unprepared questions using language sounds which a sympathetic native speaker could understand

☞ **writing**

☞ **coursework** could account for up to 40% of your marks.

USING THE TARGET LANGUAGE

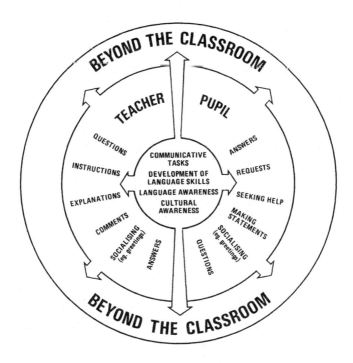

In the future it is likely that learning a modern foreign language at Key Stages 3 and 4 will look like this.

PROGRAMMES OF STUDY AND ATTAINMENT TARGETS

PROGRAMMES OF STUDY PART I:
LEARNING AND USING THE TARGET LANGUAGE

1 Communicating in the target language
2 Understanding and responding
3 Developing language learning skills and awareness of language
4 Developing cultural awareness
5 Developing the ability to work with others
6 Developing the ability to learn independently

PROGRAMMES OF STUDY PART II:
AREAS OF EXPERIENCE

Pupils must explore seven areas of experience over the period of each Key Stage. The areas of experience are:

Area A: Everyday Activities
Area B: Personal and Social Life
Area C: The World Around Us
Area D: The World of Education, Training and Work
Area E: The World of Communications
Area F: The International World
Area G: The World of Imagination and Creativity

ATTAINMENT TARGETS

AT1   Listening ● The development of pupils' ability to understand and respond to spoken language

AT2   Speaking ● The development of pupils' ability to communicate in speech

AT3   Reading ● The development of pupils' ability to read, understand and respond to written language

AT4   Writing ● The development of pupils' ability to communicate in writing

Each of the areas of study will develop a pattern of its own, but to show the kind of achievements which studying an MFL can generate, look at these possibilities.

AREA G:
THE WORLD OF IMAGINATION
AND CREATIVITY

The interest and motivation of young learners can be stimulated by themes which relate to play and leisure — themes of fantasy, fiction and fun. **Area G** — the World of Imagination and Creativity — is an area of experience in its own right, and also pervades the other AoE.

Activities might include:

Earlier we said you should not regard science as a subject in a vacuum. The same is true of modern foreign languages.

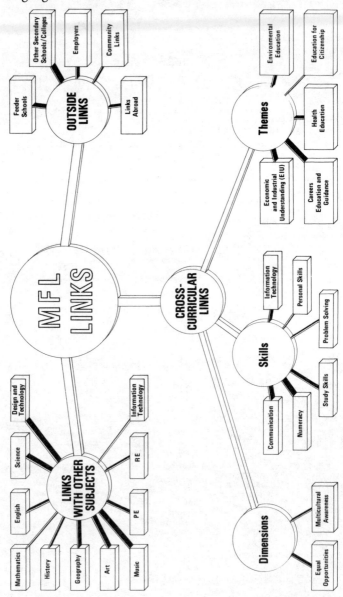

Reproduced by permission of the National Curriculum Council

Music

The **course in music** is essentially a practical one. Its aim is to provide you with extended musical experience which will improve your skills and stimulate your imagination. The course includes listening, performing and composing, and will feature music of all kinds. You will be encouraged to get behind the music to the thoughts and feelings of the composer, and you will be introduced to the skills of analysis and co-ordination which should increase your enjoyment of music.

In the exam you will be expected to:

☞ listen and respond to music, using technical and non-technical language to show you are aware of musical style and construction

☞ perform – you will be required to offer two of the following: singing or playing individually or in a group, or rehearsing and directing a group; some unprepared performance will be required

☞ compose – you will try your hand at composing during the course and this will count towards your final grade.

The essentially practical exam will include:

☞ written papers to assess the listening part of the course

☞ assessment of your genuine musical activities in the life of the school

☞ examination **test pieces.**

Know   Understand   Can do

You should note, however, that holding a grade from another music examination board will not exempt you from any part of the GCSE.

Increasingly you will find opportunities to develop skills through a number of subjects. Take information technology, for example – it has more application to Key Stage 4 music than you might at first think.

EXAMPLES OF DEVELOPING INFORMATION TECHNOLOGY CAPABILITY IN MUSIC

Communicating information	O using synthesizers, keyboards, computers, tape recorders, microphones to enable pupils to develop, organise and perform sounds O translation of sound into notations – printing notation
Handling information	O data storage of sounds – a sound bank O CD→ROM – interactive programmes developing historical knowledge O multi-tracking – recording and mixing
Modelling	O using preset forms – composing within a defined musical structure
Measurement and control	O mixing desks O 'expression' pedals/controllers O synthesis of sounds O using MIDI O sound sampling
Evaluating applications	O analysis of modern music which uses electronic means to compose and improvise O comparing live and recorded performances

Reproduced by permission of the National Curriculum Council

Physical education

Part of the National Curriculum at Key Stage 4 from 1994/5 and important to the balance of your academic studies; do not underestimate the importance of physical education in its many and various forms. Some schools may offer it to GCSE level.

AREAS OF ACTIVITY

- Athletics activities
- Dance
- Games
- Gymnastic activities
- Outdoor and adventurous activities
- Swimming

Religious studies

The **religious studies course** is open to people of all religions and to those with no religious faith at all. It is a course based on understanding rather than commitment. It will enquire into individual and group expressions of belief, trying to find out what religion is all about and show how it is reflected in what people experience, believe and do. Important life-centred questions will be asked especially in relation to the traditional attitudes and practices of various faiths. Some syllabuses will concentrate on one religion, while others will take a wider view. Moral questions will not be ignored, and the achievement of religion in shaping human beliefs and behaviour will be considered.

Know Understand Can do

In the exam you will be expected to:
- ☞ show an understanding of language, terms and ideas used in religion
- ☞ appreciate special people, writings and traditions in religion
- ☞ be clear about the main beliefs of the religion studied
- ☞ understand the pros and cons of issues
- ☞ attempt questions about the meaning of life and the variety of responses which religion gives to such questions

Know Understand Can do

☞ show you understand the difference between evidence, argument and faith.

☞ a variety of written questions from **short-answer questions** to **essays**, but you should note that you will be allowed to take copies of set texts into the exam, so your memory will not have to do overtime.

In no way will the exam test your personal faith.

☞ **coursework**, assessed by your teacher, will account for 20–30% of the marks.

Social science

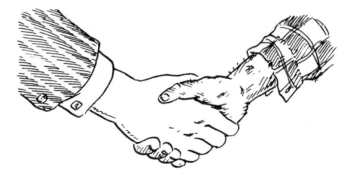

The **social science course** looks at groups of people and explores how they live, work and relate to one another.

You will study aspects of society, its economy and politics. The point of such a course is to give you a wide background against which to set your everyday experiences. Moral values also find a place in the course and you will learn to use evidence to support judgments. You will study other cultures and the course will also enable you to appreciate how society has changed. You will be trained and will gain experience in handling data.

Know	Understand	Can do	**In the exam** you will be expected to:

In the exam you will be expected to:

☞ show that you understand what today's society is like and how it has come to its present form

☞ apply that knowledge to your everyday life and changes that may occur in the future

☞ take a considered look at social, economic and political arrangements

☞ know how to use scientific methods to collect facts, analyse them and draw conclusions

☞ use language, figures and graphs to come to points of view

☞ distinguish between evidence and opinion.

The exam is likely to be based on written papers which include:

☞ material (such as photographs and newspaper cuttings) to set you thinking

☞ questions involving the use of words and figures

☞ short-answer questions and free-response essays.

☞ **Compulsory coursework** will account for at least 20% of the final mark.

To sum up

There is another way of looking at GCSEs and Key Stage 4 subjects. When you are studying them you will be developing many **skills**.

For example, in a practical science task you will be:

↦ measuring	↦ calculating
↦ experimenting	↦ drawing conclusions
↦ observing	↦ communicating.

If you start with a list of these and other skills you can plot where they are most in demand with particular subjects. Knowing yourself as you do, you could **either** make subject choices in the areas where you are most skilled **or** deliberately choose subjects that will improve skills which are most underdeveloped.

A summary of some GCSE subjects and the main personal skills you need to be successful in them Note that the absence of an * in a grid does not mean that the particular skill will never be required **Principal skills being examined**	Art and design	Design and technology	Drama
1 Calculating		*	
2 Communicating	*	*	*
3 Distinguishing between fact and opinion			
4 Interpreting creatively	*	*	*
5 Observing	*	*	*
6 Solving problems	*	*	*
7 Selecting materials	*	*	
8 Setting up experiments		*	
9 Showing an interest in the environment	*	*	*
10 Showing an interest in living things			
11 Using a language other than English			
12 Working independently	*	*	*
13 Recalling		*	*
14 Understanding yourself and others			*

Some subjects offered at GCSE

Business studies	Classical subjects	Computer studies	Economics	English	Modern foreign languages	Geography	History	Home economics	Mathematics	Music	Religious studies	Science (in combination)	Social science
*		*	*			*	*	*	*			*	*
*	*	*	*	*	*	*	*	*	*	*	*	*	*
*	*		*	*		*	*	*			*	*	*
				*			*	*		*			*
	*			*	*	*	*	*	*	*		*	*
*		*				*	*	*	*			*	*
							*	*				*	*
		*					*	*	*			*	*
*	*		*		*	*	*				*	*	*
						*					*	*	
	*	*			*				*	*			
*	*	*	*	*	*	*	*	*	*	*	*	*	*
*	*	*	*	*	*	*	*	*	*	*	*	*	*
*	*			*	*	*	*	*			*		*

7 Where Does it Lead?

It all looks so obvious. All you have to do is choose your career and fit your subjects to it. The way is marked out from before 14 through to 18, or is it?

If it were all as easy as this, there would be no need to write a book about it.

The snag is that at 14 years old, when you are doing the choosing, you may not have a clue about your future career. Only one thing is certain: by the time you are 16 you will probably be a different person – your career ideas may well have changed. The world will not have stood still either. There may be opportunities opening up which you had not dreamed of and there will be others you were relying on which may be disappearing.

Here is a list of careers you would not have considered had you left school in 1960, because they were either just beginning to appear or had not been invented.

New careers since the 1960s	
Teacher or administrator in the Open University	Oil-rig engineer in the UK
Customs and Excise officer working on VAT	Sports or recreation centre administrator
Audio engineer in stereo sound	Genetic counsellor
Hypermarket manager	Aeronautical engineer in supersonic aviation
Computer programmer	Credit-card administrator
Colour television engineer	Systems analyst
Traffic warden	Consumer protection officer
Micro-electronics engineer	Aerobics instructor
	Pet walker

Many careers that might once have seemed futuristic are emerging, but openings in them are still reasonably scarce.

Robot calibrators
Third World agro-economists
Home computer terminal engineers
Alternative technology scientists
Heliport terminal staff
Artificial food producers
Weather controllers
Data system specialists
Highway automotive controllers

How then do we cope with the unknown? How do you choose from a fixed list of subjects when your own personality and the job world are both changing? Fortunately there are certain fixed points.

1 Make sure your subject choice leaves you flexible.
2 Try to keep career doors open for as long as possible.
3 If you have a broad idea of a career make sure you cover subject requirements.
4 Be prepared to retrain and learn new skills some time in the future.

There are some subject areas which you should consider very carefully because they have a bearing now on career openings.

English

If you are aiming at a career which demands high communication skills, English at a good grade level will be a top priority. Sometimes English literature is an acceptable alternative.

Maths

A very important subject, almost as widely demanded as English. There are, however, some careers which do not demand a GCSE maths qualification of grade C or above.

History

This is not a subject which is compulsory for any career, but you should note that it is sometimes an acceptable alternative for courses which require a subject testing your command of English.

Modern foreign and classical languages

A knowledge of German can be very useful to the scientist – many technical papers are written in the language. Because Britain is now trading in the Single European Market, languages are even more important for all kinds of careers.

Computer studies

As computers are rapidly becoming everyday tools in a wide range of careers, it is important to be reasonably proficient in keyboard skills. It is *not*, however, a necessity to take GCSE computer studies which is largely a subject for those interested in computing for its own sake. Competence in information technology is more useful.

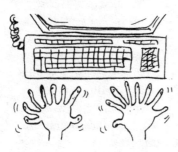

Science

Until recently science options were usually a three-way affair – a choice between the claims of physics, chemistry or biology (or perhaps a combination of two of them). There have been problems in this arrangement – not least the high proportion who drop physics and the small number of boys who take biology. This is hardly an appropriate situation for a technological society.

Balanced science may be offered in your school as a means of integrating the three elements, mixing practical skills, processes and content extracted from each of the previous scientific areas. In this way, by avoiding repetition and choosing the most relevant areas from each, it is hoped that your scientific education will be better planned and close no door in the future. It would probably take 20% of the timetable and could lead to double certification in science.

Such integrated courses dovetail into A-level and are acceptable to universities seeking a broad, balanced education, though for some science degrees, the possession of AS in the science you are not taking at A-level could be important. For those not intending to proceed to higher education it is an excellent broadly based foundation.

Business subjects

Economics is a valuable subject to understand how the present day business world works. Some schools offer a course which includes shorthand, typing, accounts and office practice. Others offer separate subjects which you can add to your choice.

Specialist areas

There are several specialist areas. Any pupil who intends to go in for one of the specialist subjects, like the creative arts, would be well advised to include the appropriate subjects at this stage.

Clearly these are important for anyone who wishes to work in an office. From a career point of view, however, you need to distinguish between the business specialism and the commercial support services. A banker is a specialist, the secretary who works in a bank provides a support service. Secretarial skills are useful, but if you are aiming to work in business as a specialist it is better to have a broad range of GCSEs than to concentrate on office skills. If you are aiming to join the support services as a typist, receptionist or clerical assistant for example, office skills are invaluable and provide a useful foundation on which to build.

Technology

A wide range of creative subjects appears under the technical studies umbrella: areas of applied technology, design studies, design and realisation, engineering workshop theory and practice, electronics, plastics, engineering and materials science. In the new exam they have been brought together under more easily recognisable names. Many of these newer courses are based on problem-solving and include project work. They provide excellent experience for everyone, not just those considering engineering as a career. These courses are also useful for those who wish to acquire the technological literacy essential to understanding the modern world.

Are some subjects more 'valuable' than others?

Teachers will say 'no'. Some employers will say 'yes'. Because they look at the question from different viewpoints it is possible for both to be right.

Teachers' point of view

Many teachers will say that all school subjects are part of human knowledge. To be good at one, therefore, is equal to being good in another. A GCSE grade C in geography is neither better nor worse than a GCSE grade C in music. The areas of study are different and cannot be compared.

Employers' point of view

Some employers and professional bodies look at GCSEs in the light of the skills they need in their businesses. For example, the personnel manager in an engineering firm may say that a GCSE grade C in science is essential and refuse to take a grade C in art into consideration. On the other hand, a higher education admissions tutor selecting potential primary-school teachers might well say that a GCSE grade C in art is just as important as one in history.

To obtain more insight into why some employers look with special interest at some subjects more than others, try the exercise on page 103, using the chart below.

Each horizontal line must add up to 20	English	Maths	Science	Modern foreign language	Humanity (eg history, geography)	Creative subject (eg art)	
Airline cabin crew							20
Barrister							20
Doctor							20
Hairdresser							20
Museum curator							20
Plumber							20
Research physicist							20
Secretary							20
Telephone operator							20
Ticket inspector							20

Talking points

1 Imagine you are an employer in each of the ten careers listed on the chart on page 102.

2 Taking one career at a time, consider the principal school subjects listed along the top.

3 Give yourself 20 points per line. Divide them up according to how important you think the subject is to the career.

4 Compare answers with a friend. Do you disagree? Why?

5 How valuable would each of the subjects in the chart be if you chose the careers listed?

What if exams are not for me?

You would not be the first to think that way. Some people can do them. Some can't.

To be unable to perform well in exams is not the end of the world. There are several points which should cheer you up if you are not a champion exam-passer.

☛ The course you follow is more important than the exam you sit at the end of it.

☛ Putting a lot of effort into subjects can be just as rewarding as getting graded at the end of the course.

☛ There are still career areas where interesting jobs need experience of certain subjects and good references rather than exam qualifications.

JOBS for which exams are **not** essential

Clerical

Typing, telephone sales, clerical and reception work. These and similar jobs are done in offices and can involve dealing with people and using simple office machinery. Your setting could be anywhere from a travel agency to a bank – big or small.

Useful school subjects
English, maths, geography, social studies

Creative

Creative jobs include music, dancing, drama, floristry, modelling and dressmaking. These jobs need flair, skill and lots of luck. In some of them you have to pass exams to obtain more responsible jobs. So you could have to face exams later on.

Useful school subjects
English and the subject that most reflects your skills

JOBS for which exams are **not** essential

Practical

This is the biggest group and the jobs call for skills which cannot be tested in exams. Sewing, machining, plastering, driving (over 18), painting and decorating, plumbing, packing, cookery, fire fighting (over 18) and many others, depending on where you live.

Useful school subjects
D&T, English, home economics, food technology, mathematics

Social

Social jobs involve meeting people and helping people. If you like doing this you could become a hairdresser, canteen assistant, shop assistant, hotel receptionist, mother's help or residential care assistant.

Useful school subjects
English, history, social studies

JOBS for which exams are **not** essential

Practical/ scientific

Farm work, gardening, cookery, machine operating and work as a care assistant are all jobs needing a background of interest in one sort of science.

Useful school subjects
Single science

Outdoor

Farm, stable and kennel work and gardening, for example, are all done out of doors. These jobs are easier to find in the country than in the town, so you may have to travel.

Useful school subjects
Single science, English, maths

8 What Shall I Need?

It is one thing to know which subjects have a bearing on a particular career and quite another to act on that knowledge. 'What shall I need?' is a question you can answer only after taking all the relevant facts into consideration. A good starting point is your career plan as it stands now, however sketchy it may be.

On the next page there are other points to check.

Check your course ahead against your career plans

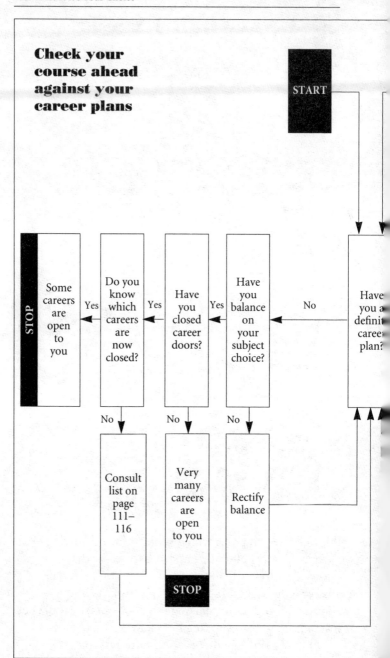

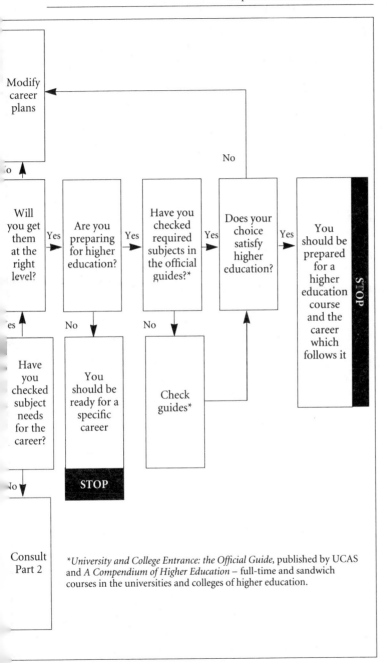

Modify career plans

o ↑

Will you get them at the right level?

Yes → Are you preparing for higher education?

Yes → Have you checked required subjects in the official guides?*

Yes → Does your choice satisfy higher education?

No

Yes → You should be prepared for a higher education course and the career which follows it

STOP

es ↑

Have you checked subject needs for the career?

No ↓

Consult Part 2

No ↓

You should be ready for a specific career

STOP

No ↓

Check guides*

*University and College Entrance: the Official Guide, published by UCAS and A Compendium of Higher Education – full-time and sandwich courses in the universities and colleges of higher education.

The simple message is that all subjects of the curriculum are important. When they are assessed together at the end of Key Stage 4 and the results announced, it is like looking at the quality of a single diamond with a collection of polished faces. No face is more important than any other, but if any one is of poor quality, it will reduce the value of the whole jewel.

We have to be realistic however. Few people are good at everything and if some grades are poor, there will be career implications. It is not easy to be precise but the lists on the next pages will give you some ideas of doors which may close on you following the announcement of GCSE results.

Don't close the doors on careers

1 Art

If you have low grades in **art** these careers may be closed to you:

Architectural technician work
Architecture
Art and design
Cartography
Landscape architecture.

2 English or English literature

If you have low grades in **English** or **English literature**, these careers may be closed to you:

Accountancy*
Accounting
Actuarial work
Advertising
Air piloting*
Air traffic control*
Army officer*
Astronomy*
Audiology technician
    work
Baking technology
Banking and building
    society work
Beauty therapy
Brewing technology*
Cardiology technician
    work
Chiropody
Civil Service clerical
    assistant
Civil Service clerical
    officer
Civil Service executive
    officer
Company secretaryship*
Customs and Excise work
Dental therapy work
Dietetics
Dispensing optics
Environmental health*
Estate agency and
    auctioneering
Exporting

Fashion design and
    production
Forestry
Geology
Health services
    management
Home economics
Horses, work with
Housing management*
Insurance
Interpreting and
    translating
Journalism*
Landscape architecture*
Legal executive work
Legal work – solicitor
Librarianship
Local government
    administration
Marketing
Mathematics
Medical laboratory
    science work
Medical records work*
Merchant Navy deck
    officer and radio officer
Meteorology
Midwifery*
Neurophysiology
    technician work
Nursery nursing
Occupational therapy
Ophthalmic optics

Organisation and
methods and work
study
Orthoptics*
Osteopathy*
Personnel work
Photography*
Physiotherapy
Printing technology
Public relations
Purchasing and stock
control
Radiography/radiotherapy

Recreation
administration
Royal Air Force officer
Royal Navy officer
Speech therapy*
Surveying
Teaching*
Town planning*
Trading standards
administration
Travel work
Veterinary nursing work.

* English grade C or above required

3 Modern foreign languages

If you have a low grade in a **modern foreign language**,
these careers may be closed to you:

Archive work
Diplomatic Service
Interpreting and translating
Patents
Speech therapy.

4 Geography

If you have a low grade in **geography**, these careers may
be closed to you:
Cartography (preferred)
Landscape architecture.

5 Mathematics

If you have a low grade in **mathematics**, these careers
may be closed to you:

Accountancy
Accounting
Actuarial work
Advertising
Air piloting
Air traffic control
Architectural technician
    work
Architecture
Army officer
Astronomy
Audiology technician
    work
Baking technology
Banking and building
    society work
Biochemistry
Biology
Brewing technology
Broadcasting (technical)
Building technician and
    technology work
Cardiology technician
    work
Cartography
Chemistry
Computer programming
Dentistry
Design
Dietetics
Dispensing optics (or
    pharmaceuticals)
Economics
Engineering
Environmental health
Estate agency and
    auctioneering

Fashion design and
    production
Food science and
    technology
Forestry
Geology
Health services
    management
Horticulture
Information science
Insurance
Landscape architecture
Leather technology
Local government
    administration
Market research
Marketing
Materials science
Mathematics
Medical laboratory
    science work
Medical records
    work
Medicine and surgery
Merchant Navy deck
    officer
Merchant Navy
    engineering officer
Merchant Navy radio
    officer
Metallurgy
Meteorology
Midwifery
Neurophysiology
    technician work
Operational research
Ophthalmic optics

Organisation and
  methods and work
  study
Orthoptics
Patents
Personnel work
Pharmacy
Photography
Physics
Plastics and rubber
  technology
Printing technology
Psychology
Public relations
Purchasing and stock
  control
Quarrying
Radiography/
  radiotherapy

Recreation
  administration
Royal Air Force officer
Royal Navy officer
Speech therapy
Statistics
Surveying
Surveying technician
  work
Teaching*
Textile technology
Town planning
Trading standards
  administration
Travel work
Veterinary work.

*Mathematics grade C or above required

6 Single and double sciences

If you have low grades in **science**, these careers may be
closed to you:

Air piloting
Air traffic control
Animal nursing auxiliary
Animal technician work
Archaeology
Architectural technician
  work
Architecture
Astronomy
Audiology technician
  work

Baking technology
Beauty therapy
Biochemistry
Biology
Brewing technology
Broadcasting (technical)
Building technician and
  technology work
Cardiology technician
  work
Chemical engineering

Chemistry
Chiropody
Dairy technology
Dental hygiene work
Dental therapy work
Dentistry
Dietetics
Dispensing assistant/pharmacy technician work
Dispensing optics
Dyeing
Engineering
Environmental health
Farming (some levels)
Fashion design and production
Food science and technology
Forestry
Geology
Hairdressing
Home economics
Horticulture
Information science
Laboratory technician work
Landscape architecture
Leather technology
Materials science
Medical laboratory science work
Medicine and surgery
Merchant Navy deck officer
Merchant Navy engineering officer
Merchant Navy radio officer
Metallurgy
Meteorology
Midwifery
Museum work
Nature conservation
Neurophysiology technician work
Nursing
Occupational therapy
Operational research
Ophthalmic optics
Orthoptics
Osteopathy
Patents
Pharmacy
Photography
Physics
Physiotherapy
Printing technology
Psychology
Quarrying
Radiography/ radiotherapy
Recreation administration
Speech therapy
Surveying
Surveying technician work
Teaching
Textile technology
Trading standards administration
Veterinary work.

Opening doors to careers later

However, there are ways of opening doors to careers later.

1 By sitting special tests or examinations set by employers or professional bodies as alternatives to public exams.

2 Aiming higher than a 16+ entry into a given field, eg graduate entry, which would bypass GCSE required subjects.

3 Mature entry (over 21 years of age). Mature students who apply for a place on a university or training course may not have to satisfy the normal academic requirements. When older people who do not have the normally required number of GCSEs apply for a job, employers will often take their experience into consideration instead. Many careers are open to mature entrants.

Resolving those clashes

If you are forced into a choice you are not happy about, look around for ways of compensating.

For example

Can't take typing?	Look around for evening classes (but make sure you get the head-teacher's permission)
Clashes with music?	Try lessons or groups out of school
Art or drama not possible?	How about a school art club or extra-curricular drama?
Language clash?	Are there evening classes?

Some subjects at GCSE are offered again in the sixth form. Others can be bypassed at GCSE but still studied to A-level. There is often more flexibility than first appears.

9 Looking into the Future

The courses you are taking for the next two years should be enjoyable, but the exams are not just there for the fun of sitting them. They measure your performance and prepare the way for the next stage.

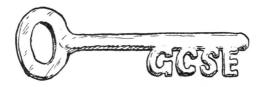

Think of GCSE grades as keys which will open some doors. The difficulty is that you are not yet sure which doors you will want to open. Therefore you don't know which keys to choose. Obviously the bigger the bunch, the more doors you will be able to open.

Let's start with the doors. There will be a number of them facing you in two to four years' time.

We will look at each one in turn and examine the ways of opening it.

A-Levels

Which subjects will I need if I go on to GCE Advanced level?

You may know already that you want to go on to take your A-levels. You may even know which subjects you would like to take.

Different institutions make different arrangements, though most normally require you to have gained a GCSE grade A–C in order to allow you to take a subject at A-level. Often they prefer you to have gained at least a GCSE grade B to begin an A-level subject. Just occasionally it may not be possible to take a subject at GCSE that you are likely to want to study at A-level. Remember, though, that it is important for everyone to complete a GCSE course in English, mathematics and a science. Find out from your teachers what happens in your local sixth form or college.

Don't just concentrate on subjects you know you will

need at A-level. Later on, a college offering higher education courses (ie at 18+) will want to see evidence of study in breadth and depth, and Key Stage 4 of the National Curriculum should ensure that this occurs.
For the future scientists, a GCSE grade A–C in a language and the humanities is important now. For those inclined to the humanities, a GCSE grade A–C in science is vital at this stage.

It is important, however, to remember that in some subjects, particularly science and languages, the A-level work follows on from the GCSE work. These are subjects in which you develop your knowledge step by step and they are obviously more difficult to take up again once you have given up on them.

You should also be prepared to consider seriously the opportunities offered by the post-16 vocational A-levels the Advanced GNVQs (General National Vocational Qualifications) (see page 130).

If you don't know what subjects you want to do at A-level or GNVQ, don't worry. There is no need to make up your mind at this stage. The National Curriculum at Key Stage 4 is designed to provide a broad range of GCSE subjects which will give you the chance to decide which ones you might like to study further. You can make the decisions about AS/A-level subjects and GNVQs during Year 11. Some sixth forms, colleges and further education establishments will allow you to read for a combination of AS/A-levels and GCSEs, as well as GNVQs.

Improving and extending GCSEs after 16

Whether or not you can take GCSEs after the age of 16 can only be answered by individual schools and colleges. Traditionally, sixth forms have been geared to A-levels, but recently sixth-form courses have been designed for 16+ exams, vocational studies and AS/A-levels. Most students are prepared to take their GCSEs at the end of Year 11, some are ready earlier, some later, some may be recommended not to sit them at all. There are people who come back to subjects they dropped at school and sit exams many years later. We don't all develop in the same way or at the same speed. It might be a very good thing to stay on at school into the sixth form for GCSEs. Talk to your teachers; ask their advice. There will also be many post-16 colleges which offer GCSE courses.

In addition, many colleges of further education offer courses at GCSE which are directed in certain areas – such as a pre-business studies GCSE programme, a pre-art and design GCSE programme – and many others centred on a general vocational area. These enable you on completion to have the option to go on to AS/A-levels or to take up a vocational course directly related to a particular area of work and employment.

Resitting

It may be vital for your career plans to resit certain exams in which your grades were not good enough. You may be pleased to know that coursework done for an exam in Year 11 can be offered again for your retake (given that you are satisfied with it). Many students prefer to submit coursework which they have produced during their retake year. (The present trend is for most GCSE subjects to be at most 40% coursework and 60% examination based, though there is a tendency to reduce this to 20:80.)

> ! It is always useful to know you can have a second chance, but don't allow it to lull you into a false sense of security.
> ! Retaking some subjects could prevent you studying others because of the way the timetable works.

Extending your GCSEs

One reason for continuing at GCSE level after 16 is to gain better grades in subjects which are important to your future but in which you did not fare so well first time round. Another reason is to study new subjects which were not previously offered on your timetable at Key Stage 4.

These new subjects might be:

Communication studies	**Sociology**
Government, politics and law	**Russian**
	Media studies
Photography	**Health studies**
Psychology	**Geology**

Most of these subjects are related to particular career fields. Courses in them can be very useful; they give you the chance to sample the subject and make up your mind whether you want to pursue a career in it.

Some schools and colleges run a one-year post-16 course with experience of work. You spend one day a week or a block of weeks in industry or in a local further education college gaining industrial experience or beginning a basic, specialist course before leaving full-time education. Many colleges build experience of work into GCSE courses and most students will have had the opportunity of a placement in work, usually of two weeks' duration, during Key Stage 4.

Search

1 Find out what the post-16 arrangements are in your school area.
2 Are there any subjects you must have before you can go on to the next stage?
3 Use your school or college careers library, your careers teacher and your careers officer to help you gain long-term information.

GCSEs and the world of work

Employers make their own use of GCSE results in the selection of new employees. Not all your GCSE subjects will be relevant to the job you have applied for, but your overall choice of subjects, your grades as well as what sort of person you are, will be a very useful guide to a prospective employer. Look at the extract below provided with the permission of Cornhill Insurance.

Getting into Cornhill	Comment
Educational qualifications	
At Cornhill we prefer people with **either**	
(a) a GCE in two subjects at A-level, and two at GCSE level.	post-16 courses are relevant
These passes must include English	note the essential GCSE subject
or	
(b) any three passes in GCE at A-level	subject freedom post-16
or	
(c) the National Certificate or National Diploma in Business and Finance.	an alternative route

We do, however, realise that not everybody is able to stay in full-time education until the age of 18; or pursue part-time courses such as the National Certificate. If you haven't reached this level you will spend more time in training in Cornhill and your part-time studies will take a bit longer. We therefore also consider applications from people with at least

you **can get in at 16, *but...***

(d) four subjects at GCSE grades A–C, including English and a mathematical subject, which will enable them to study for the National Certificate.

two subjects are now essential

These qualifications are linked to the requirements of the Chartered Insurance Institute, whose qualifying examination is the professional examination of the insurance industry. You must check the acceptability of your particular subjects from the Examination Handbook of the Chartered Insurance Institute, copies of which are freely available from the Institute at 31 Hillcrest Road, South Woodford, London E18 2JP.

NB Those professional bodies!

some checking to do

Two quick points

☞ You may apply before your exam results are known.

always a good idea

☞ Equivalent Scottish qualifications are equally acceptable.

Academic qualifications are not everything – they just set the minimum educational level required. The different jobs at Cornhill make their particular demands, but throughout Cornhill it is essential to have a good command of English, both in conversation and on paper. You should not be frightened of figures ... but generally it is only simple arithmetic that is required! In a firm with such variety of business it is important to be quick thinking and flexible in your approach. You need to be interested in what is going on around you and have sufficient curiosity to assemble the facts on which to base balanced judgments. Persistence too will help; studying for qualifications part-time is not easy, and you must be well motivated and well organised in order to succeed.

Thank goodness! But that does not mean that a cheerful face and a glib tongue will make up for a woolly brain

GCSEs and youth training

In September 1983 the government introduced the Youth Training Scheme (YTS), not just to keep the unemployed busy but to provide training for all young people aged

16+ hoping to go into industry. It is now known as Youth Training (YT) and is on the one hand designed to give broad vocational training, and on the other to provide a pool of people with experience of work and skills from which to recruit. Some YT courses will have GCSE entry requirements, so it is not true to say that exams don't matter when there is little work about!

Whichever world of employment you choose, the principle remains the same. Employers will use:

☛ public examination results
☛ your character reference
☛ your Record of Achievement

to sift out candidates for interview.

If you arc 13, GCSEs may seem to you like the buffers at the end of the line. For many there will be a junction on this line which goes a long way further.

How youth training (YT) operates

Youth training is a planned programme of approximately two years' work experience and training. Its aims are to give you competence in a range of skills and the ability to apply your skills in different situations, to have confidence in yourself and your ability and to gain recognised vocational qualifications.

In most parts of the country YT is available in nearly all areas of work, including administrative and office work, health and community care, hairdressing, sales work, science, catering, agricultural work, building, engineering, garage work, printing and others.

YT is open to all 16 and 17 year-old school-leavers and, in theory, all 16 and 17 year-olds are guaranteed a place on YT. However, in the current economic situation it has proved impossible to place all YT applicants in work. It is a mix of on- and off-the-job training and all programmes must offer young people the opportunity to obtain re-cognised vocational qualifications to a minimum standard;

normally this will be NVQ level 2 (see page 129).

Young people may be either employed or non-employed on YT and many traditional apprenticeships, such as those in the building trades, motor mechanics, engineering and hairdressing, have been fully integrated within YT. YT has become the usual – and often the only – route into these jobs.

Your local Careers Service office is likely to publish a booklet giving details of YT programmes available in your area. Remember, a weekly trainee allowance is paid to you and this opportunity exists regardless of your gender, race or ability.

Many employers now recruit through YT, some offering fully paid jobs with YT, but others have not joined the scheme and they will continue to offer employment including, in some cases, associated day release for further education. If at the end of Year 11 you do not intend to continue in full-time education you will need to consider whether it will be better for you to apply for permanent employment immediately or whether you should apply for a YT place.

What are the implications for subjects in Key Stage 4?

☞ Some training will involve complex technical skills, so selection based on school examinations may occur.

☛ Some employers or industrial groups may recruit only those who have been on their training scheme.

☛ Not all who take a training scheme will land a job at the end of it. There is no guarantee of work so get as many qualifications as you can while you are still at school; they will be invaluable.

☛ The old established routes of GCSE/A-levels in school or college will still be available.

☛ The better your 16+ qualifications, the stronger will be your position to choose.

GCSEs and vocational qualifications in work

As an alternative to GCSEs and AS/A-levels you can, after Year 11, go on to follow a vocational route. This is a programme or course which leads to a qualification linked with a particular area of work (hairdressing and beauty, leisure and tourism, engineering, art and design, science, computing and others).

Vocational qualifications are available at different levels to match with GCSEs, AS/A-levels and higher education qualifications (degrees and diplomas).

To ensure that vocational qualifications at specific levels can be compared with each other (that is, that they have similar standards) and to help companies recognise the levels, all qualifications relating to work are now becoming National Vocational Qualifications (NVQs). The most used levels for 16+ are levels 2 and 3.

NVQs are set out in the form of 'competencies' – 'can do' statements – and a particular group of competencies become a 'unit'.

Qualifications can be gained either by completing all the units for a whole NVQ or credit can be given for individual units. These credits can be used towards other qualifications or for employment.

NVQ levels

NVQ level	Description	Broadly equivalent to
Higher 5	Profession, Middle management	Higher education
Higher 4	Higher technician, Junior management	Higher education
Intermediate 3	Technician, Advanced craft, Supervisor	2+ A-levels (or equivalent in AS)
Foundation 2	Basic craft	4+ GCSEs A–C awards

GCSEs and full-time vocational studies after 16

By the time you reach 16+ there will be new opportunities to take full-time vocational studies which are different from the NVQ competencies secured while at work. These are courses leading to GNVQs (General National Vocational Qualifications) at Intermediate and Advanced levels and can be taken in schools and colleges. They are more fully discussed in the companion book to this, *Decisions at 15/16+*. At this stage you just need to know that they exist and understand briefly what this kind of study can offer.

GNVQ subjects

GNVQs are available in the following areas:

- Art and Design
- Business
- Health and Social Care

- Leisure and Tourism
- Manufacturing.

By the time you have finished your GCSEs, the following areas of study will also be available:

- Science
- Construction and the Built Environment
- Catering and Hospitality
- Information Technology
- Engineering Technology
- Media/Communications/Performing Arts
- Agriculture/Environment
- Distribution
- Management.

GNVQ studies cover many aspects of the world of work, but they approach occupational areas in a broader way than NVQs. GNVQs explore business and industry and introduce you to the processes involved, while helping you gain the basic skills essential to your personal development and future success. The assignments increase your knowledge of a chosen area and may provide valuable work experience.

You may wish to study for a GNVQ at either Intermediate or Advanced level. An Intermediate GNVQ is valued as highly as four GCSEs at grade C or above. This gives you an idea of the amount of work and the difficulty involved. An Advanced GNVQ is thought of as highly as two A-level passes.

Structure
GNVQ studies allow you to undertake your studies in manageable amounts and let you retake parts of the course if it becomes necessary. The principal features are:

- modular units (self-contained blocks of study)
- credit accumulation (which means you can move

between institutions or interrupt your studies and
still qualify)
- working at your own pace
- planning your course with your teacher
- help and guidance throughout
- studies possible at different levels to university
  entrance level
- tests can be taken as many times as you like to
  improve your score.

Results

GNVQs assess what you know, understand and prove you
can do. It is the outcome of your studying which is
important (your Portfolio of Evidence). The level of your
result, which can be pass, merit or distinction, is also
dependent on your ability to plan and evaluate your work
independently.

GCSEs and higher education

The 18+ stage probably looks a long way off. It is not too
early, however, to take a look, if only to check out the
relation between **GCSE and university and colleges of
higher education.**

First of all, remember that when you apply for a college or
university place, you will be doing it from the
first year in the sixth form. You will have started on your
A-level or GNVQ (General National Vocational
Qualification) course but your academic track record will
be based on your GCSE qualifications. When you
complete your application form they, together with your
predicted grades, are entered as your representatives who
will speak on your behalf, so they had better be good!

But 16+ exams have a more precise duty to do as far
as universities and colleges of higher education are

concerned. There are two kinds of qualifications you need
to possess:

Entry qualifications	**+**	Faculty or departmental qualifications

☞ Entry qualifications
These are basic qualifications to be obtained before the
university or college will accept you to study anything.
☞ Faculty/departmental requirements
These are special subjects relevant to your proposed

course of study required by the faculty or department you wish to join. These subjects will vary from department to department.

For example

You wish to go to Barchester University to read medicine.

You must satisfy the requirements in the left-hand column in the table below to go to Barchester at all. If you wish to read medicine there, you must also satisfy the particular subjects which the admissions tutor for medical students requires to ensure that all students on the course have good foundations in science which are necessary to progress on the course.

University of Barchester	
General requirements to study any course at the university	**Course requirements for medicine**
Five GCSE subjects at grades A, B or C, including English, mathematics or a science and two GCE A-levels or a BTEC or GNVQ	Three A-levels, one in chemistry and two from biology, physics and mathematics. The subject not held at A-level must be held at GCSE grades A, B or C or a good BTEC or GNVQ in science

These are the minimum requirements but competition for places is fierce and in practice a school-leaver would be expected to have at least six well-balanced GCSEs at grades A, B or C taken at one sitting and at least two good A-levels or a good BTEC or GNVQ. The rather low minimum requirements allow universities to take individual circumstances into account.

Generally speaking, the wider your range of subjects, the broader your choice of higher education courses.

Search

☞ *University and College Entrance: The Official Guide* Published by the University and College Admissions Service (UCAS), PO Box 67, Cheltenham, Gloucestershire GL50 3SE. It is available in schools, libraries and careers offices.

A point to think about

A degree course is not usually a training for a career; it is an academic education. Many arts graduates' careers have little connection with their degree subject. For instance, a history graduate may enter a marketing training scheme with a large company. They would not be using history directly at all. Companies often run graduate training schemes which offer higher starting salaries and better promotion prospects than a school-leaver could expect. There are also graduate training schemes in the Civil Service, the armed services, local government administration and the police. In some cases a degree course is training for a specific profession and the profession is open only to graduates of these courses (for example architecture, dentistry, medicine, ophthalmic optics, pharmacy and veterinary science). However, if you hold a degree in one of these subjects you do not have to enter the profession.

GCSEs and Records of Achievement

Examination results do not tell the whole story. People who train and employ 16 year-olds are no longer satisfied with the rather narrow picture that exam results give – they only indicate academic ability. Of course this is important, but how successful an employee you are likely to be also depends on the kind of person you are.

School reports as we used to know them have mostly been replaced by a profiling system which is done by you as well as your teacher. An example of a young person's Record of Achievement in mathematics in the first half of Year 10 is shown on the next page.

Thus, when completed, your Record of Achievement, whether a local or the National Record of Achievement, is a document you can take with you which highlights your skills and abilities both in and out of school. It should be a help in planning your future because it summarises your achievements at school, your qualifications, your activities, any jobs and experiences of work you have had and contains a personal statement written by you.

The National Record consists of four sections:

The Personal Record
The Action Plan
The Assessment Record
Certificates.

Your National Record should help you to plan your future as well as show what you have already achieved.

MANOR COMMUNITY COLLEGE
RECORD OF ACHIEVEMENT

MATHEMATICS

NAME: Laura Prentis   10 MU

COMMUNICATION SKILLS

PUPIL COMMENT: I think that I'm quite a good communicator both orally and in writing. I think that I have understood well all the mathematical language which I have come across so far. I think that my presentation in my work books is quite good.

TEACHER COMMENT: Your progress is excellent with very good results in your last two tests. Your written work is well presented, you are well organised and oral work is very thoughtful.

PROBLEM SOLVING SKILLS

PUPIL COMMENT: I enjoy problem solving because each problem is different. I like the way we have the choice of how to set our work out and our results. ie graphs, tables etc. I find some easy and some hard, I find the harder ones better as they are more of a challenge.

TEACHER COMMENT: Your work in this area is sound. You analysed the task well and were able to use this analysis to solve most of the problem. At the end your work on predicting future behaviour was a bit weak.

AGREED TARGET:

To maintain my present rate of progress.

Laura Prentis   F. Murphy   DATE: 22.01.92.

At the present time, based on our assessment of your attainment, we think you are likely to be entered for G.C.S.E. at the following level:

FOUNDATION	INTERMEDIATE	HIGHER
☐	☐	✓

If you would like further information about the National Record of Achievement ask your teachers or careers adviser or write to:

The Employment Department
N705
Moorfoot
SHEFFIELD
S1 4PQ.

☛ Achievement recording is also something you can do. Collect all the evidence from sources in and out of school that have something valuable to say about you.

---

eg

music awards
swimming certificates
school commendations
athletic achievements
guide/scout awards
evidence of club membership
first-aid certificates
activity photographs
competition awards
interesting letters
records of special achievements

Mount everything carefully in a non-stick photograph album and you will have something interesting to take with you when you go for an interview.

Leisure education

Sounds like time to put your feet up! Not quite, but there could be periods ahead when you have more time on your hands than you expect.

☞ Unemployment remains a fact of life that will not go away. If there is a time when it is hard to find work, you will have unexpected time to spare.

☞ Job-sharing is likely to become more common. This means you work half a day and a partner works the other half. This results in more time at your disposal.

☞ The age of retirement may come down.

☞ Thanks to medical science, people are living longer.

Your generation may have more leisure time than any previous generation and this could affect your course choices.

Are there subjects which could help you become a more skilful homemaker?

Consider: social studies, cookery, textiles, etc.

Are there subjects which could lead to a club activity?

Consider: drama, music, art, geography, history.

Are there subjects which would enable you to offer a service?

Consider: typing, accounts, office practice.

Are there subjects which would help you care for others?

Consider: home economics, first-aid, biology, community service.

It's a fresh way to look at subject choice and one which could have lasting importance.

Common abbreviations

Careers books can baffle with abbreviations. Here is a list of the more common ones you are likely to meet.

A-level	A two-year academic course focused on one subject designed to follow on from GCSEs. Most students take two to four A-levels and good grades (A–C) are the entry requirement for higher education
AS	An AS is roughly half the work of an A-level
BTEC	Business and Technology Education Council
D&T	Design and technology is one of the subjects under the technology umbrella and is a foundation subject

CGLI	City and Guilds of London Institute (an examining body for vocational courses)
CRAC	Careers Research and Advisory Centre
GCSE	General Certificate of Secondary Education
GNVQ	General National Vocational Qualification
MFL	Modern foreign language
NVQ	National Vocational Qualification
RSA	RSA Examinations Board (an examination body for certain vocational courses)
SCAA	School Curriculum and Assessment Authority
TEC	Training and Enterprise Council
UCAS	University and College Admissions Service
YT	Youth training

10 Getting Help

No one pretends that it's easy to make decisions about one's future. There are so many unknowns. You won't know if you like a subject, or if you are any good at it, until you've studied it. You can't know exactly which subjects you'll need four years from now.

This is why help is important. Nobody should feel that they have to get on with it by themselves. Most schools have particular staff whose job it is to make sure the issues are clear, and who will spend a good deal of time making sure you know what you are doing.

Different people will give advice from different points of view. It is important to understand their point of view when discussing problems with them.

Who is available to help you with your decisions?

Talk to:
Form teacher or tutor who sees you in an all-round school situation.

Talk to:
Careers officers and careers teachers who give you independent, unbiased advice on the various choices you will have to make.

Talk to:
College staff who can advise upon routes through further education which will enable you to obtain specialist qualifications.

Talk to:
Employers who can offer you advice based upon their experience of business and industry in the light of employment needs and training opportunities.

Talk to:
Subject teachers who provide an objective view of your subject abilities.

Talk to:
Parents who know you best of all as a person.

There will be plenty of things to talk over with them for you will be seeking to achieve a compromise between:
- ☞ what you like
- ☞ what you are good at
- ☞ what you are recommended to do
- ☞ what you need.

What should you discuss with your advisers?

☞ Like

It would be nice if you liked all your school subjects, but probably you don't. Remember that likes and dislikes are often determined by who teaches you. Is it sensible to choose subjects on that basis? You will probably be taught by someone else next year anyway. Is it the way of learning that makes a subject popular? Fieldwork, projects, a visual approach, experiments? What really triggers likes and dislikes?

☞ Good at

Are you good at the things you like? Do you always like the things you are good at? How soon should you specialise in your best subjects? Can this be carried too far? Could you drop some of your good subjects for two years and then take them up again? What are the skills which make you good at a subject anyway?

☞ Recommended

Who recommends you to do what? Do your parents and teachers give conflicting advice? How can you sort out objective and subjective viewpoints? Have you a good balance of subjects and methods of working? Are you carrying too many subjects that rely heavily on your memory?

☞ Need

How far ahead have you looked? Does your choice allow you sufficient flexibility? What changes might occur in the career field that interests you? If changes come, will you be able to adapt to them? Where can you get advice on questions like these?

Like   **Good at**

Your Subject Choice

 Need   **Recommended**

within the framework of what is required

11 Making the Choice

Now comes the crunch. After all the reading, talking, finding out and discussion, the choice has to be made. And only you can make it. You have the information you need; now you just draw it all together. Use the chart on pages 148–149 to set out the possibilities.

Using the chart

On the top of the chart are the main subject families. A well-balanced choice will include subjects from each family. Write in all the subjects you *can* include for Key Stage 4 on the '**Offered**' level.

Along the **'Required'** line put a tick in each subject box which you are required to do within the National Curriculum. Against **'Like'** put a tick in the box for every subject you like. Against **'Good at'** tick the subjects you are reasonably good at. Against **'Recommended'** tick the subjects that your teachers have recommended you to take for GCSE. Against **'Need'** tick the GCSE subjects required for any special career you are interested in.

When you have completed the chart look at the overall picture it presents. The pattern of ticks will be a useful guide when you make your final choice.

	English			Science		Modern foreign languages		
	English language	English literature	Mathematics	Single science	Double science			
Offered								
Required								
Like								
Good at								
Recommended								
Need								
Final Choice								

Humanities		Technology			Creatives			Other	

Footnote 1

We wish you every success both with making your decisions for your Key Stage 4 courses, as well as with the subjects themselves when the courses begin.

We suggest you keep referring to this Student Helpbook:

☛ to keep up to date with your thinking about careers by using the information in Part 2
☛ throughout Key Stage 4.

Michael Smith
Veronica Matthew

Footnote 2

Answer to the outdoor pursuits problem on page 19

The object of the exercise was to achieve a balance between comfort, enjoyment and safety. The more you take, the more comfortable you will be at camp but the more you will regret it during the day. The ideal limit is about 13.5 kg, but note you must be prepared for some unexpected situations. Allowing for the worst possible weather the following choice would be ideal:

rucksack with dustbin liner
sleeping bag
lightweight tent with sewn-in groundsheet
waterproof outer clothing
stove/fuel
matches
survival bag
first-aid kit
emergency rations
spare clothing (perhaps socks and a light tracksuit)
food to last two days

map of the area to be covered
compass
whistle
torch
completed route card
water container

Clothing to be worn
boots
anorak
sweater
woollen socks
woollen-based trousers (not jeans!)
woollen-based shirt
gloves

Note
If you were to climb Ben Nevis in January, you would
need extra and different gear.

12 Where Can I Find Out More?

Working In series. This is the main series of careers booklets published by the Careers and Occupational Information Centre (COIC). After each career in the 'Careers Guide', reading has been recommended and in most cases it includes a booklet in this series. The price quoted in the 'Careers Guide' does not include postage. You will also find COIC's *Occupations '94* useful to look at. The address to write to is: The Careers and Occupational Information Centre, Sales Department, Moorfoot, Sheffield S1 4PQ.

The Penguin Careers Guide by Anna Alston and Anne Daniel (consultant editor Ruth Miller) is an excellent general careers book published by Penguin.

Job Book. Published for CRAC by Hobsons Publishing PLC, Bateman Street, Cambridge CB2 1LZ. This annual publication gives details of the opportunities offered by British employers to those entering employment, from school-leavers at 16 with or without GCSEs to postgraduates. Your careers teacher or co-ordinator should have this.

Decisions at 15/16+. Published for CRAC by Hobsons Publishing PLC, Bateman Street, Cambridge CB2 1LZ. A guide to the decisions facing the 15 year-old.

Decisions at 17/18+. Published for CRAC by Hobsons Publishing PLC, Bateman Street, Cambridge CB2 1LZ. A sixth-former's starting point for thought and discussion with parents, teachers and careers advisers on the range of choice after A-levels.

GNVQ: is it for you? Published for CRAC by Hobsons Publishing PLC, Bateman Street, Cambridge CB2 1LZ. A student's guide to the new General National Vocational Qualifications. It explains what is involved in a GNVQ programme of study and the value of this vocational qualification.

Excellent free fact sheets on BTEC courses are available from the Publications Despatch Unit, Business and Technology Education Council, Central House, Upper Woburn Place, London WC1 0HH (please specify the level of the course you are interested in and the occupational area).

Free information on RSA courses can be obtained from The RSA Examinations Board, Westwood Way, Cambridge CB4 8HS.

The Compendium of Higher Education is a comprehensive guide in two volumes. Volume I covers degree courses in universities (old and new); volume II covers non-degree higher education courses. They are published by the London and South-Eastern Regional Advisory Council for Further Education (LASER), 21 Bedford Square, London WC1B 3HH.

The Advisory Councils publish lists of all part-time, sandwich and full-time courses in their area.

ACER (East Anglia), Merlin Place, Milton Road, Cambridge CB4 4DP

EMFEC (East Midlands), Robins Wood House, Robins Wood Road, Aspley, Nottingham NG8 3NH

NCFE (Northern), 5 Grosvenor Villas, Grosvenor Road,
Newcastle upon Tyne NE2 2RU

CENTRA (North West), The Town Hall, Walkden Road,
Worsley, Manchester M28 4QE

SRCET (Southern), The Mezzanine Suite, Civic Offices,
Reading RG1 7TD

SWAFET (South West), Bishops Hull House, Bishops
Hull, Taunton, Somerset TA1 5RA

YHAFHE (Yorkshire and Humberside), The Business and
Media Centre, 13 Wellington Road, Dewsbury WF13 1XG

Welsh Joint Education Committee, 245 Western Avenue,
Llandaff, Cardiff CF5 2YX

The UCAS Handbook. Published by the University and
College Admissions Service (UCAS), PO Box 67,
Cheltenham, Gloucestershire GL50 3SF, obtainable free
from schools, colleges and local careers offices.

University and College Entrance. Published by the
University and College Admissions Service (UCAS).

CRAC Degree Course Guides series. Thirty-five
comparative first-degree course guides titled by degree
subject; they are revised every two years, half in alternate
years. Published for CRAC by Hobsons Publishing PLC,
Bateman Street, Cambridge CB2 1LZ.

Directory of Further Education. Comprehensive guide to
further education courses leading to formal qualifications

in the UK. Published for CRAC by Hobsons Publishing PLC, Bateman Street, Cambridge CB2 1LZ.

The NATFHE Handbook of Initial Teacher Training. Lists courses in education for intending teachers. National Association of Teachers in Further and Higher Education. Obtainable from Linneys Colourprint, 121 Newgate Lane, Mansfield, Nottinghamshire NG18 2PA.

Guide to the Colleges and Institutes of Higher Education. Published by the Standing Conference of Principals. Obtainable from Mr G R Mann, Administrative Officer, Standing Conference of Principals, Edge Hill College of Higher Education, Ormskirk, Lancashire L39 4QP.

2

Careers Guide

Careers Guide introduction

This guide is based on a survey of degree and professional requirements that was carried out in June 1992 and revised in October 1993. Entry requirements are changing all the time so it is important to check with the individual colleges and the professional bodies.

Under each career the different entry routes are listed, together with the certificate and diploma courses that can be taken and the GCSEs required.

The phrase 'A good base of GCSEs' is often used for careers where higher education at a university or college of higher education is essential. This normally means that successful candidates will have at least six academic GCSEs at grades A, B or C including English, mathematics, a modern foreign language, science and two other academic subjects.

Many careers listed here have less formal entry routes. You probably have older friends and relatives who have no diplomas and certificates but are doing well in their careers. The routes you will find in the 'Careers Guide' are the authorised ones, and are recommended to anyone who wants to be professionally secure.

Accountancy

An accountant checks the company accounts and advises companies on financial matters, such as tax and record-keeping systems. Accountants work in public authorities, companies or firms of accountants.

☛ Full-time, sandwich and part-time courses at colleges or by an open-learning or correspondence course for the preliminary, professional and final examinations of the Chartered Association of Certified Accountants. Two A-levels and three GCSEs at grades A, B or C in five distinct subjects are required, including English and mathematics. Only one of the GCSEs may be in a craft subject. Minimum age 18. Three years' relevant accountancy experience is required for candidates for the associateship. The relevant practical experience may be obtained in private practice, industry, commerce or the public sector. The foundation course is not compulsory.

☛ Study leave to prepare for the examinations of the Institute of Chartered Accountants in England and Wales is provided as part of a training contract with an authorised training office. Most training is available in firms of accountants and increasingly in industrial or commercial organisations. At least two A-levels and three GCSEs at grades A, B or C are required. English and mathematics must be included at either level. All subjects are acceptable. Graduates complete a three-year training contract. Non-graduates usually take a one-year accountancy foundation course at an approved university or higher education college and then spend four years working in an office under a training contract.

☛ Full-time, sandwich and part-time courses at college for all four stages of the examinations of the Chartered Institute of Management Accountants. Three GCSEs at grades A, B or C, including English and mathematics, and two A-levels are required. All subjects are acceptable.

Candidates for the associateship must be at least 21 and have three years' practical experience.

☛ Full-time, part-time and hybrid courses at college for both foundation and professional examinations of the Chartered Institute of Public Finance and Accountancy for which three GCSEs at grades A, B or C and two A-levels, including English and mathematics at either level, are required. GCSEs in child development, drama, photography and textiles are not acceptable. The foundation course is compulsory for non-graduates. Those taking the professional examinations must be employed in a financial position by a public authority.

☛ Full-time or part-time college courses for a BTEC National Certificate/Diploma in Business and Finance. Four GCSEs at grades A, B or C, preferably including English and mathematics, or a BTEC First Certificate/Diploma are required for entry. A BTEC National award is accepted as an alternative to two A-levels for entry to the courses leading to the professional examinations.

☛ Entry after higher education: see GCSEs and higher education on page 132. The majority of students entering training to become accountants are graduates.

✍ **Further information** Chartered Association of Certified Accountants, 29 Lincoln's Inn Fields, London WC2A 3EE

Institute of Chartered Accountants in England and Wales, Chartered Accountants' Hall, Moorgate Place, London EC2P 2BJ

Chartered Institute of Management Accountants, 63 Portland Place, London W1N 4AB

Chartered Institute of Public Finance and Accountancy, 3 Robert Street, London WC2N 6BH

▥ **Reading** *Working In* series: *Accountancy* published by and available from the Careers and Occupational Information Centre, price £2.50

☛ School careers library classification NAB

Accounting technician work

Accounting technicians are the support staff on whom the professional accountants rely. In small companies they work on their own, keeping the day-to-day accounts.

☛ Two-year full-time, three-year part-time, open-learning or correspondence courses for the new practical assessments of the Association of Accounting Technicians. These assessments, which test competencies, have replaced the examinations and lead to National Vocational Qualifications (NVQs) at Levels 2–4. There are no fixed entry requirements but you will need to demonstrate that you are both literate and numerate. For candidates direct from school this will mean around four GCSEs at grades A, B or C, including English and a numerate subject such as mathematics or principles of accounts.

☛ Two-year full-time or three-year part-time college courses for the BTEC National Certificate/Diploma in Business and Finance followed by study for the Association of Accounting Technicians' final examinations. Four GCSEs, preferably including English and mathematics, or a BTEC First Certificate/Diploma are required for entry to a BTEC course.

In addition, a period of approved working experience is required for membership of the Association of Accounting Technicians. Students should register with the Association before starting their course.

✍ **Further information** Association of Accounting Technicians, 154 Clerkenwell Road, London EC1R 5AD

▥ **Reading** *Qualifying as an Accounting Technician* published by and available free from the Association

☛ School careers library classification NAB

Acting
see **Drama**

Actuarial work

Actuaries apply statistics to life assurance, pension schemes and other insurance problems. For example, they might work out the life assurance premiums for different age groups according to their life expectancy.

☛ Correspondence course for the examinations of the Institute of Actuaries while working in an office under a qualified actuary. Three GCSEs at grades A, B or C, including English or English literature, and two A-levels are required. One of the A-levels must be at least grade B in a mathematical subject or at least grade C in further mathematics or higher mathematics. The other A-levels should be at least grade C. All subjects are acceptable.

☛ Entry after higher education: see GCSEs and higher education on page 132. The majority of students entering training to become actuaries are graduates.

✍ **Further information** Institute of Actuaries, Napier House, 4 Worcester Street, Oxford OX1 2AW

▥ **Reading** *Becoming an Actuary* and *What is an Actuary?* published by and available free from the Institute

☛ School careers library classification NAJ

Administration
see **Civil Service** *and* **Local government administration**

Advertising

After studying the products or services to be advertised, the advertiser will prepare advertisements and place them in newspapers and magazines, on TV and radio as well as on hoardings.

☞ Full-time or part-time college courses for BTEC
National Certificate/Diploma in Business and Finance.
Four GCSEs at grades A, B or C, preferably including
English and mathematics, or a BTEC First Certificate/
Diploma are required for entry. These can be followed
either by a course for a BTEC Higher National Certificate/
Diploma or by study for the Communication, Advertising
and Marketing Education Foundation (CAM) Certificate.
☞ Two years' part-time evening and home study for
CAM Certificate in Communication Studies. The subjects
studied are marketing; advertising; public relations;
media; research and behavioural studies; sales promotion
and direct marketing. All students must be over 18. They
must have three GCSEs at grades A, B or C and two
A-levels, or five GCSEs at grades A, B or C and have been
employed in a relevant field for one year; English GCSE
must be included, or a BTEC National
Certificate/Diploma in Business and Finance.
☞ Entry after higher education: see GCSEs and higher
education on page 132.
✍ **Further information** The Communication,
Advertising and Marketing Education Foundation (CAM
Foundation), 15 Wilton Road, London SW1V 1NJ
☞ School careers library classification OD

Aeronautical engineering
see **Engineering**

Agriculture
see **Farming and agricultural advisory work**

Air cabin crew

Air cabin crew look after the needs of passengers on
board a plane, serving meals and selling duty-free goods.
In emergencies it is the responsibility of the cabin crew to
ensure the safe evacuation of passengers.

☛ On-the-job training including a course of several weeks at a training centre. A good general education with some GCSEs, not necessarily at grades A, B or C, is required. Nursing, catering, social welfare or receptionist experience is an advantage. The most useful GCSE subjects are English, geography, mathematics, food and nutrition and foreign languages. Minimum age on most airlines is 20. Candidates have usually had another job before they apply.

✍ **Further information** Aviation Training Association, 125 London Road, High Wycombe, Buckinghamshire HP11 1BT

☛ School careers library classification YAB

Air Force
see **Royal Air Force**

Air piloting

Pilots are responsible for all aspects of flying an aeroplane. On larger aircraft two or three pilots may work together, sometimes with a flight engineer. Apart from working for airlines, pilots spray crops, make test flights and aerial surveys and give flying instruction.

☛ Full-time courses of approximately 70 weeks are undertaken at approved training schools at Oxford, Perth, Trent (Cranfield) and the British Aerospace Flying College (Prestwick) for the Commercial Pilot's Licence (Aeroplanes) with Instrument Rating. Nine-month full-time courses at approved training schools at Cranfield, Redhill, Prestwick and Oxford for the Commercial Pilot's Licence (Helicopters). Five GCSEs at grades A, B or C are required, including English, mathematics and a single science award which must include physics. A-levels may be needed for sponsorship.

☛ Entry after higher education: see GCSEs and higher education on page 132.

For all courses entrants must be medically fit.
Minimum age on qualifying for a professional pilot's
licence is 18. The course fees and expenses are over
£50,000, but a student may arrange sponsorship.
✍ **Further information** Civil Aviation Authority, FCL4,
Aviation House, South Area, Gatwick Airport South, West
Sussex RH6 0YR
Aviation Training Association, 125 London Road, High
Wycombe, Buckinghamshire HP11 1BT
☞ School careers library classification YAB

Air traffic control

Air traffic controllers direct the taking off, landing and
movement of air traffic in UK airspace by giving radio
messages to pilots while watching aircraft movements on
a radar screen.
☞ Two-year college course and on-the-job training for
student air traffic controllers. Five GCSEs at grades A, B
or C, including English and mathematics, and two
subjects studied at A-level are required. All subjects are
acceptable.
✍ **Further information** Civil Aviation Authority,
Personnel Recruitment Section, Room T820, CAA House,
45–59 Kingsway, London WC2B 6TE
▥ **Reading** *A Career in Air Traffic Control* published by
and available free from the Civil Aviation Authority
☞ School careers library classification YAB

Ambulance service work

Ambulance crew attend to seriously ill and injured people
and give initial medical aid before transporting them to
hospital. Their more routine work, patient transport
service, includes taking infirm people who cannot use
public transport to treatment centres.
☞ On-the-job training with part-time study for
examinations. Candidates for entry to the ambulance

service must pass a medical test and preference is given to candidates with GCSEs. Minimum age 21, cadets 16 years.

✍ **Further information** Ambulance Service Headquarters, address from the local telephone directory

📖 Reading *Working In* series: *Emergency Services* published by and available from the Careers and Occupational Information Centre, price £2.50

☛ School careers library classification JOC

Animal nursing
see **Veterinary nursing**

Animal technician work

Animal technicians breed and care for animals in laboratories. They ensure the animals have the highest standards of care. This is a job for people who like working with animals and are interested in science. You cannot do this job unless you love animals, but a mature regard for them is needed, not just sentimentality.

☛ On-the-job training with day-release for the Institute of Animal Technology's examinations. A GCSE at any grade in a subject demonstrating facility in English and a GCSE at grades A, B or C in mathematics or a science subject or BTEC units in these subjects are required.

☛ Part-time study while employed in a laboratory for the BTEC National Certificate in Science (animal technology options). Four GCSEs at grades A, B or C, including mathematics and a science subject, or a BTEC First Certificate/Diploma are required for entry.

✍ **Further information** Institute of Animal Technology, 5 South Parade, Summertown, Oxford OX2 7JL

📖 Reading *Working In* series: *Animals – Work With* published by and available from the Careers and Occupational Information Centre, price £2.65

☛ School careers library classification QOX

Antique dealing
see **Retail and wholesale distribution**

Archaeology

Archaeologists study past people by the scientific analysis of material remains. These remains can be very varied – they may be prehistoric burial mounds, Roman forts, medieval villages or World War II defences.

☛ Higher education is virtually essential for entry; see GCSEs and higher education on page 132. Useful GCSEs include foreign languages, history, geography, chemistry and other science subjects, and mathematics. There is some work for which higher education is not required but this is rarely a long-term career.

✍ **Further information** Council for British Archaeology, 112 Kennington Road, London SE11 6RE Council for British Archaeology, Northern Office, King's Manor, York YO1 2EP

▥ **Reading** *Careers in Archaeology* published by and available free from the Council for British Archaeology, please send a large stamped addressed envelope

☛ School careers library classification FAH

Architectural technician work

Architectural technicians work closely with architects and other members of the building team. Their work involves preparing working drawings, making surveys, collecting information, inspecting work at a building site and applying computer-aided design techniques.

☛ Three-year part-time course for the BTEC National Certificate in Building Studies. Four GCSEs at grades A, B or C, preferably including science, mathematics and a subject testing command of English, or a BTEC First Certificate/Diploma in Construction are required for entry.

☛ To become a full member of the British Institute of Architectural Technicians the BTEC National Certificate should be followed by the BTEC Higher National Certificate in Building Studies (Architectural) and then two years of practice qualification.

✍ **Further information** British Institute of Architectural Technicians, 397 City Road, London EC1V 1NE

▥ **Reading** Careers leaflets published by and available free from the Institute

☛ School careers library classification UB

Architecture

Architects design buildings; they must consider the technical specifications as well as the final appearance of the building.

☛ An architect cannot practise in the UK without registering with the Architects' Registration Council of the United Kingdom (ARCUK). Higher education is essential (see GCSEs and higher education on page 132). RIBA guidance for minimum requirements is three GCSEs at grades A, B or C, including English, mathematics and single award science, and at least two A-levels. The two A-levels must be in academic subjects and some colleges specify mathematics. Some aptitude for drawing is required and colleges usually wish to see a portfolio, although GCSE or A-level art is not generally formally required.

✍ **Further information** Royal Institute of British Architects (RIBA), 66 Portland Place, London W1N 4AD

▥ **Reading** *A Career in Architecture* published by and available free from the Royal Institute of British Architects
Architecture, Landscape Architecture and Planning Degree Course Guide, published for CRAC by Hobsons Publishing PLC, price £4.99

☛ School careers library classification UB

Archive work

Archivists maintain collections of documents in record offices run by local authorities, central government and a variety of private and other institutions.

☛ Higher education is essential; all the entrants are graduates from a variety of degree subjects; a postgraduate diploma in archive administration is essential. GCSEs in subjects such as history, geography, modern languages and Latin are useful. See GCSEs and higher education on page 132.

✍ **Further information** Society of Archivists, Information House, 20–24 Old Street, London EC1V 9AP

▥ **Reading** *Archives as a Career* published by and available free from the Society of Archivists

☛ School careers library classification FAG

Army

National defence is the main task of all branches of HM Forces. Today's Army is trained in the use of the most sophisticated weapons and equipment.

Officer entry (men and women)

☛ Scholarship scheme for sixth-form study at schools with facilities for A-level studies. Age limits 16 years – 16 years 6 months.

☛ Welbeck College provides a two-year sixth-form science-based course preparing boys for a regular commission in a Technical Corps. Candidates must have at least five GCSEs at grades A, B or C, including English, mathematics and double award science. Age limits 15 years 9 months–17 years 6 months.

☛ Regular Commissions: three GCSEs at grades A, B or C and two A-levels are required including, at either level, English, mathematics and either single award science or a foreign language. Age limits 17 years 9 months – 25. (Some corps requiring specialist qualifications will accept candidates up to 27.)

☞ Short Service Commissions: five GCSEs at grades A, B or C, including English, are required. Certain subjects are required for technical arms. Age limits 17 years 9 months – 25. (Some corps requiring specialist qualifications will accept candidates up to 27.)

☞ Graduate-entry officers may be awarded Regular Commissions or Short Service Commissions. See GCSEs and higher education on page 132. The Army can award cadetships to students in higher education; there is also a bursary scheme.

Adult soldiers
☞ Any fit British subject who passes certain selection tests can serve as a soldier. Age range 17–25.

Junior entry
☞ Entry as apprentices, junior bandsmen and junior leaders, the upper age limit is 17 years 6 months. Certain selection tests must be passed.

✍ **Further information** For officer entry: DAR1, Ministry of Defence, Empress State Building, Lillie Road, London SW6 1TR

For soldier and junior entry: DAR2, Ministry of Defence (address as above)

▥ **Reading** A range of publications is available from Army Careers Information Offices

☞ School careers library classification BAF

Art and design

The demand for full-time artists who produce sculpture, paintings and limited editions of prints is extremely small. Designers, however, apply their creative ability to develop a wide range of products. Some designers, such as silversmiths, potters and jewellers, also work as craftspeople making their own products, while other designers work as part of a team for the mass production of furniture, ceramics, electrical equipment, clothing, footwear and textiles. Other designers create exhibitions, displays and all types of printed material.

Degree courses

☛ Degree courses in art or design last three years and students specialise in graphic design, three-dimensional design, fine art or textile/fashion design. It is possible to specialise within three-dimensional design: taking industrial design (engineering), furniture, ceramics, interior design or theatre design. Students with three GCSEs at grades A, B or C and two A-levels, or with one GCSE at grade A, B or C and three A-levels, can enter the degree course without taking a one-year foundation course. A foundation course, however, is recommended for all students.

Non-degree courses

☛ Two-year full-time or equivalent part-time college programme for the BTEC National Certificate/Diploma in Design. Four GCSEs at grades A, B or C or a BTEC First Certificate/Diploma in Design are required for entry. Students will have to show samples of practical work displaying evidence of potential practical and creative ability.

☛ Two-year full-time or equivalent part-time programme for the BTEC Higher National Certificate/Diploma in Design. For entry either a BTEC National Certificate/Diploma in Design, a foundation course or, exceptionally, one A-level is required.

☛ Vocational courses, which last from one to four years, are available in a wide variety of subjects and entrance requirements vary from evidence of a good general education to the possession of up to five GCSEs at grades A, B or C. For many vocational courses a year's foundation course is not necessary. Vocational courses lead to college diplomas, City and Guilds certificates or professional qualifications such as those of the British Display Society.

☛ Two-year full-time course for the National Diploma advanced level of the British Display Society in either retail display or point of sale, exhibition, prestige and services followed by a year's practical employment and the final level examination of the Society. Three GCSEs at grades A, B or C are required, including one subject that gives evidence of the use of English. Candidates must also submit evidence demonstrating potential practical and imaginative ability. All subjects are acceptable. The British Display Society offers BTEC National Diploma and Higher National Diploma holders special category membership.

✍ **Further information** The Design Council, 28 Haymarket, London SW1Y 4SU (not careers in fine art) British Display Society, 70A Crayford High Street, Dartford, Kent DA1 4EF (display and promotional design only)

National Society for Education in Art and Design (NSEAD), The Gatehouse, Corsham Court, Corsham, Wiltshire SN13 0BZ

📖 **Reading** *Careers in Design* published by and available free from the Design Council, please enclose a large stamped addressed envelope

Design Courses in Britain also published by the Design Council, price £6.95

Guide to Courses and Careers in Art, Craft and Design published by and available from NSEAD, price £12.15 including postage

Working In series: *Art and Design* published by and available from COIC, price £2.50

☛ School careers library classification E

Astronomy

Astronomers study the planets, stars and galaxies by applying physics, chemistry, biology, meteorology and many other disciplines.

☛ A degree in astronomy or a closely related subject is essential. A good base of GCSEs which will enable you to take mathematics and physics at A-level is recommended.

✍ **Further information** Education Committee, British Astronomical Association, Burlington House, Piccadilly, London W1V 9AG

▥ **Reading** *Becoming a Professional Astronomer* published by the British Astronomical Association, price 40 pence including postage

☛ School careers library classification QOF

Auctioneering
see **Estate agency, auctioneering and valuation**

Audiology technician work

Audiology technicians perform a wide variety of tests of hearing and fit and maintain hearing aids.

☛ Two-year part-time course leading to the BTEC National Certificate in Physiological Measurement while working in the National Health Service. Four GCSEs including English, mathematics and double award science are required.

✍ **Further information** British Association of Audiology Technicians, Mrs M Marshall, Cottage Street Hearing Centre, Brierley Hill, West Midlands DY5 1RE

▥ **Reading** *Employment and Training of Audiology Technicians* published by and available free from the British Association of Audiology Technicians – please send a large stamped addressed envelope

☛ School careers library classification JOB

Baking technology

Baking technologists apply their scientific training to the preparation, storage and selling of biscuits, cakes, pies and bread.

☛ Full-time or part-time college courses for the BTEC National Certificate/Diploma in Science (Baking Technology). Four GCSEs at grades A, B or C, preferably including at least a single award science, mathematics and a subject testing command of English, are required for entry.

☛ Entry after higher education: see GCSEs and higher education on page 132.

✍ **Further information** Federation of Bakers, 20 Bedford Square, London WC1N 4AA

☛ School careers library classification SAC

Banking and building society work

The high street banks run accounts and the system of cheques. They give advice on investments and promote trade by giving loans and overdrafts. Their other services include foreign exchange and help with financial matters when someone dies. The merchant banks mainly deal with finance for companies. Building societies lend money on mortgage to people who wish to buy their own homes. They also maintain accounts in a similar way to bank accounts, but are not members of the cheque clearing system.

☛ Part-time courses for the BTEC National Certificate/Diploma in Business and Finance while working in a bank or building society. Four GCSEs at grades A, B or C, including English and preferably mathematics, or a BTEC First Certificate/Diploma are required for entry.

☛ Part-time study for the three-year Chartered Institute of Bankers' Banking Certificate while working in a financial institution. No entry qualifications are required for the preliminary section (one year); for the final section the candidates must have passed three papers in the preliminary section or hold one or more A-levels or its equivalent and

English GCSE at grades A, B or C. Arrangements can be made at schools for pupils in the senior classes to study and sit the examinations of the preliminary section of the Banking Certificate using computer-assisted learning packages.

☛ Part-time study for the one-year Chartered Institute of Bankers' pre-Associateship course. At least one A-level and GCSE English are required for entry.

☛ The BTEC courses, the Banking Certificate and the pre-Associateship course can be followed by study for the Chartered Institute of Bankers' Associateship examinations.

☛ Entry after higher education: see GCSEs and higher education on page 132.

✍ **Further information** The Chartered Institute of Bankers, 10 Lombard Street, London EC3V 9AS. The Chartered Building Societies Institute has recently merged with the Chartered Institute of Bankers.

▥ **Reading** *Working In* series: *Money Business* published by and available from the Careers and Occupational Information Centre, price £2.50

☛ School careers library classification NAD

Barrister, the Bar
see **Legal work**

Beauty therapy and consultancy

Beauty therapists treat both the face and the body. They may give facials or massage customers and remove unwanted hair by wax or by electrolysis. Beauty consultants work in shops helping customers to choose cosmetics.

Beauty therapists
☛ Full-time and part-time courses for which three to five GCSEs at grades A, B or C, including English and at

least single award science, are generally required. For some courses one A-level is also required. Minimum age is usually 18.

Beauty consultants

☛ On-the-job training while working in a department store or for a cosmetic company. Some GCSE subjects (not necessarily at grades A, B or C) are sometimes required. English and mathematics are particularly useful subjects.

☛ Full-time and part-time courses for which two GCSEs at grades A, B or C are generally required.

📖 **Reading** *Working In* series: *Hairdressing and Beauty* published by and available from the Careers and Occupational Information Centre, price £2.95

☛ School careers library classification IL

Biochemistry

Biochemists usually work in laboratories studying the chemistry of living things. They can work in the food and drug industries, in agricultural and medical research and in hospitals.

☛ Entry after higher education: see GCSEs and higher education on page 132. A good base of GCSEs at grades A, B or C will be required for future specialisation in science A-levels.

For entry as a biochemistry technician see Laboratory technician work

✍ **Further information** Biochemical Society, 59 Portland Place, London W1N 3AJ

📖 **Reading** *Careers for Biochemists* published by and single copies available free from the Biochemical Society *Biochemistry Degree Course Guide* published by Hobsons Publishing PLC, price £4.99

☛ School careers library classification QOM

Biology

Biologists study plants, animals and micro-organisms.
☛ Part-time, sandwich or full-time college courses for
the BTEC National Certificate/Diploma in Science
(Applied Biology). Four GCSEs at grades A, B or C,
preferably including double award science, mathematics
and a subject testing command of English, or a BTEC First
Certificate/Diploma in Science are required for entry.
☛ Part-time, sandwich or full-time college courses for
the BTEC Higher National Certificate/Diploma.
Applicants must hold a BTEC National Certificate/
Diploma in Science with certain units or have studied
biology and either chemistry or a physical science to
A-level and passed in one of these.
☛ If from the outset you are planning to be a
professional biologist you should aim to take a degree
course. A good range of GCSEs at grades A, B or C,
including mathematics and double award science, is
required with A-levels in science subjects.
✍ **Further information** Education Department,
Institute of Biology, 20 Queensberry Place, London
SW7 2DZ
▥ **Reading** *Careers with Biology* published by and
available from the Institute of Biology, price £2.90
including postage
Career leaflets are obtainable free from the Institute
provided a large stamped addressed envelope is sent
Biological Sciences Degree Course Guide published by
Hobsons Publishing PLC, price £4.99
☛ School careers library classification QOD

Bookbinding
see **Printing – printing crafts**

Bookselling
see **Retail and wholesale distribution**

Botany
see **Biology**

Brewing technology

Brewing technologists are in charge of the biological processes of malting barley and brewing beer.

☛ Part-time, sandwich or full-time college courses for the BTEC National Certificate/Diploma in Chemistry or Biology. Four GCSEs at grades A, B or C, including mathematics and preferably a double award science, or a BTEC First Certificate/Diploma in Science are required for entry.

☛ Part-time, sandwich or full-time courses for the BTEC Higher National Certificate/Diploma in Chemistry or Applied Biology. For the chemistry courses candidates must hold a BTEC National Certificate/Diploma with certain relevant units or A-level chemistry and evidence of substantial study beyond GCSE of mathematics and physics. For the biology courses candidates must hold a BTEC National Certificate/Diploma with certain relevant units or have studied biology and either chemistry or a physical science to A-level and have passed in one of these.

☛ Part-time study for the examinations of the Institute of Brewing. Three GCSEs at grades A, B or C, which must include English and mathematics, and two science A-levels are normally required from candidates who have had an English education.

☛ Entry after higher education: see GCSEs and higher education on page 132. The most suitable degree courses would be in biochemistry, biology, chemistry or chemical engineering. There are a few specialised degree and postgraduate courses in brewing science. A good base of GCSEs at grades A, B or C is required for specialisation, in subjects such as mathematics, chemistry and physics, or biology at A-level.

✍ **Further information** The Institute of Brewing,
33 Clarges Street, London W1Y 8EE
☛ School careers library classification SAC

Bricklaying
see **Building crafts**

Broadcasting: radio and television

There are many careers in the BBC and the commercial
television companies that are dealt with elsewhere in this
book – careers such as library work, computing, graphic
design, film and video producing, secretarial work and
hairdressing. On the technical side of broadcasting there
are technical operators and engineers.

Technical operators are divided into three main
categories: (i) sound; (ii) camera; and (iii) post-
production recording operators. There are also some jobs
that are multidiscipline, eg news and current affairs
technical operators. GCSE standard in mathematics,
science and English is required. Equally important is a
genuine interest in and knowledge of a relevant area, eg
microphones, tape recorders, photography and the visual
arts. All applicants must be over 18 and have normal
hearing and colour vision.

Trainee engineers service and repair the technical
equipment. The minimum requirement is three GCSEs at
grades A, B or C in mathematics, science and English; and
mathematics and physics studied to A-level or a BTEC
National Certificate/Diploma in Electronic Engineering.
A practical interest in electronics is an advantage.
Applicants should be over 18 with normal hearing and
colour vision. The BBC also recruits a number of
graduates each year with non-technical degrees to follow
a training programme similar to that of the trainee

engineer. Applicants must have GCSE mathematics at grade A, B or C.

Engineers usually have qualifications in electrical engineering or in telecommunications. They have either been trainee engineers or enter with a BTEC Higher National Certificate/Diploma or a university or college of higher education degree (see Engineering).

Production work generally requires applicants to have relevant experience; this can include journalism, the arts or theatre. Although no specific qualifications are requested, most applicants have a good track record educationally and a strong interest in radio and television output. Educational subject choice can be as wide as the topics that fill radio and TV programmes! Increasingly jobs are advertised on a short-term contract basis (three months to a year). Competition for jobs is keen.

The BBC offers a limited number of training opportunities in production and journalism. Jobs and training opportunities open to newcomers are advertised in the national press and a summary appears on CEEFAX page 696.

✍ **Further information** BBC Corporate Recruitment Services, PO Box 7000, London W12 7ZY

BBC Engineering and Technical Operations Recruitment, 201 Wood Lane, London W12 7TS

Commercial television companies: for addresses see telephone directories

▥ **Reading** *Working In* series: *TV, Film and Radio* published by and available from the Careers and Occupational Information Centre, price £2.95

☞ School careers library classification GAL

Building crafts

Bricklayers build walls with bricks and blocks using a trowel and mortar.

Carpenters and joiners work with wood, making and

fitting doors, window frames, staircases and floorboards. Many items are made in a factory nowadays and fitted on site.

Heating and ventilation workers install heating and air conditioning systems, mainly in factories and office blocks.

Painters and decorators paint inside and outside a building and put up wallpaper.

Plasterers prepare and apply plaster to inside walls and ceilings. Sometimes they also apply renderings to outside walls.

Plumbers put water systems in new buildings, as well as repairing them in existing buildings. Sometimes they install heating systems in houses.

Thermal insulation workers lay mineral wool in the roof and lag pipes (this is often carried out by other craftspeople).

Wall and floor tilers fix tiles to the floors and walls inside buildings.

Roof tilers and slaters fix tiles and slates to roofs after covering the rafters with roofing felt.

In many small building firms a building craftsman or woman undertakes a number of different crafts.

☛ No requirements are laid down nationally but many employers will give preference to candidates with GCSEs at grade E or above in English, mathematics, science and technology for their apprenticeship vacancies.

☛ The Construction Industry Training Board is the principal managing agent for the construction industry for the Youth Training (YT) Scheme. To a large extent YT has replaced the apprenticeship entry to building crafts. Training will take place in a college or training centre as well as at the workplace. Trainees will work towards the new National Vocational Qualifications (NVQ) as they become available.

✍ **Further information** Careers Advisory Service, Construction Industry Training Board, Bircham Newton, King's Lynn, Norfolk PE31 6RH

Ⅲ Reading *Careers in Construction* is published by and available free from the Construction Industry Training Board
Working In series: *Construction* published by and available from the Careers and Occupational Information Centre, price £2.35
☛ School careers library classification UF

Building surveying
see **Surveying**

Building technician and technologist work

Building technicians and technologists work in the offices of larger building companies and on building sites. They supervise the work, co-ordinating the various types of craft worker, ensuring that deadlines are respected and standards are maintained.
☛ Full-time, part-time and sandwich college courses for the BTEC National Certificate/Diploma in Building Studies. Four GCSEs at grades A, B or C or a BTEC First Certificate/Diploma in Construction are required for entry.
☛ Full-time, part-time or sandwich courses for the BTEC Higher National Diploma/Certificate in Building Studies. Entrants should have either a BTEC National Diploma/Certificate or four GCSEs at grades A, B or C, including mathematics, a double award science and a subject testing command of English, and mathematics and physics studied to A-level with a pass in either. The BTEC Higher awards and appropriate experience can lead to associate membership of the Chartered Institute of Building.
☛ Part-time study for the examinations of the Construction Surveyors' Institute. Four GCSEs at grades

A, B or C are required. Mathematics, English and at least a single award science are the preferred subjects. Students should be in approved employment and/or following an approved course.

☛ Entry after higher education: see GCSEs and higher education on page 132. Degrees in building are often four-year sandwich courses and require a good base of GCSEs at grades A, B or C for specialisation in mathematics and physical sciences at A-level. Degree holders with appropriate experience can apply to become members of the Chartered Institute of Building.

✍ **Further information** Careers Advisory Service, Construction Industry Training Board, Bircham Newton, King's Lynn, Norfolk PE31 6RH

Chartered Institute of Building, Englemere, King's Ride, Ascot, Berkshire SL5 8BJ

Construction Surveyors' Institute, Wellington House, 203 Lordship Lane, London SE22 8HA

▥ **Reading** A range of booklets is published by and available free from the Construction Industry Training Board

☛ School careers library classification UD

Butchery
see **Retail and wholesale distribution**

Buying
see **Retail and wholesale distribution**

Cardiology technician work

Cardiology technicians set up and operate equipment for diagnosing and treating heart disease. They often operate machines which produce an ECG (electrocardiogram) of a patient. They are present during open heart surgery and cardiac pacing providing records and measurements for the physician or surgeon.

☛ Two-year part-time day-release or block-release courses for the BTEC National Certificate in Science with physiological measurement options. Four GCSEs at grades A, B or C are required for entry, including English, mathematics and at least a single award science. This may be followed by the BTEC Higher National Certificate in Physiological Measurement.

✍ **Further information** Society of Cardiological Technicians, 2 Poplar Avenue, Windlesham, Surrey GU20 6PL

▥ **Reading** *Medical Technical Officers & Assistants (HSC 13)* published by the Department of Health and available free from Health Service Careers, PO Box 204, London SE5 7ES

☛ School careers library classification JOB

Careers work

Careers officers advise young people and adults on their choice of career, training opportunities and further education courses.

☛ One-year or two-year part-time training courses for people with suitable experience in teaching, industry, commerce, social work or public administration. Places at training centres are normally awarded only to those who hold recognised professional qualifications or a degree or who have had five years' relevant experience and meet the academic standard.

✍ **Further information** The Local Government Management Board, Arndale House, Arndale Centre, Luton LU1 2TS

Institute of Careers Guidance, 27a Lower High Street, Stourbridge, West Midlands DY8 1TA

▥ **Reading** *A Career as a Careers Officer* and *Training for the Careers Service* available free from the Institute of Careers Guidance

☛ School careers library classification KED

Carpentry
see **Building crafts**

Cartography

Cartographers prepare maps from information provided by land surveyors and are increasingly able to make detailed interpretation from aerial photographs and remotely sensed imagery. Most of the posts are in the Ordnance Survey, other government departments or with local authorities, a few with commercial map publishers and the exploration departments of oil companies. The career is in the process of rapid change with the increasing use of computers and geographical information systems.

☛ Day-release courses for the BTEC National Certificate/ Diploma in Surveying (Cartography). Four GCSEs at grades A, B or C or a BTEC First Certificate/ Diploma are required for entry. The BTEC National awards can be followed by the BTEC Higher National Certificate/ Diploma.

☛ Entry after higher education: see GCSEs and higher education on page 132. Some degree courses in geography include cartography. Entry requirements are a good base of GCSEs at grades A, B or C, preferably including mathematics, a science and a foreign language, leading to A-levels including geography and mathematics. Mathematics, computer science and engineering graduates may also be recruited for cartography.

✍ **Further information** Establishment Officer, Ordnance Survey, Romsey Road, Southampton SO9 4DH

▥ **Reading** *Careers in Cartography* single copies available free from R W Anson, Principal Lecturer in Cartography, Oxford Brookes University, Gipsy Lane, Headington, Oxford OX3 0BP, provided a large stamped addressed envelope is sent

☛ School careers library classification UT

Catering, including hotel and institutional management

Caterers prepare and serve food in hotels, restaurants, factories, schools and colleges.

Institutional managers provide food and accommodation in hostels, college halls of residence and similar places.

Hotel managers run hotels and restaurants.

Management and supervisory posts

☞ Full-time and part-time college courses for a BTEC National Certificate/Diploma in Hotel, Catering and Institutional Operations. Four GCSEs at grades A, B, or C or a BTEC First Certificate/Diploma are required for entry. The BTEC National awards can be followed by the BTEC Higher National Certificate/Diploma. The Higher award courses can also be entered with three GCSEs at grades A, B or C and one A-level, including English or a subject testing command of English and either mathematics or a subject testing numeracy or a biological or physical science.

☞ Two-year part-time course for the Hotel, Catering and Institutional Management Association's (HCIMA) Certificate. Four GCSEs at grades A, B or C are required, including a subject testing command of English and a subject such as mathematics demonstrating numeracy. At least a single award science would be desirable. The BTEC National awards or the Certificate can be followed by a one-year full-time sandwich or three-year part-time or distance learning course for the HCIMA's Diploma. Corporate membership of the HCIMA is open to those who have passed the Diploma examination or an equivalent and have had two years' appropriate experience.

☞ Entry after higher education: see GCSEs and higher

education on page 132. Several universities and colleges of higher education run degree courses in hotel and catering management. The entry requirements vary but it would be advisable to include in your GCSE subjects English, French, mathematics and double award science.

Hotel reception, cookery, domestic service and allied careers

☛ Full-time and part-time college courses leading to National Vocational Qualifications (NVQs) in housekeeping, reception, food preparation and cooking, food and drink service, etc. The Hotel and Catering Training Company provides training programmes leading to NVQs in a variety of different careers. Some colleges require GCSEs with at least grade D or E in some subjects.

✍ **Further information** Hotel, Catering and Institutional Management Association, 191 Trinity Road, London SW17 7HN

Hotel and Catering Training Company (HCTC), International House, High Street, Ealing, London W5 5DB

▥ **Reading** *Working in the Hotel and Catering Industry* published by HCTC and Macmillan, price £7.99

Working In series: *Hotel and Catering* published by and available from the Careers and Occupational Information Centre, price £2.65

☛ School careers library classification IB

Ceramics
see **Art and design**

Ceramics technology
see **Materials science and metallurgy**

Chemical engineering
see **Engineering**

Chemistry

A chemist studies the elements which compose all matter, applying his or her knowledge to fields as diverse as synthetic fibres, fertilisers and pharmaceuticals. One word of warning: the person who works in a chemist's shop preparing drugs is a pharmacist and not a chemist!

☛ Full-time or part-time college courses for a BTEC National Certificate/Diploma in Science. Four GCSEs at grades A, B or C, including mathematics and preferably double award science, or a BTEC First Certificate/ Diploma in Science are required for entry. Possession of a BTEC National Certificate or Diploma would lead to technician posts.

☛ Three-year sandwich or two-year full-time course for the BTEC Higher National Diploma in Science (Chemistry). An A-level in chemistry and evidence of substantial study beyond GCSE level of a related subject (colleges would normally expect this subject to be mathematics or physics) or a BTEC National Diploma/Certificate with specified units are required for entry. Eligible students on a BTEC Higher National Diploma course may elect to take an additional paper for Graduate Membership Part I of the Royal Society of Chemistry. This may be followed by study for the Part II examinations of the Society.

☛ Most professional chemists have taken a degree in chemistry. See GCSEs and higher education on page 132. A good base of GCSEs at grades A, B or C is required and A-levels in mathematics, chemistry and physics should be taken, although some flexibility in A-level subjects is allowed.

✍ **Further information** Royal Society of Chemistry, Burlington House, Piccadilly, London W1V 0BN

▥ **Reading** *Chemistry – Life beyond Exams* published by and single copies available free from the Royal Society of Chemistry

Chemistry Degree Course Guide published by and available from Hobsons Publishing PLC, price £4.99
☞ School careers library classification QOB

Chiropody

Podiatry is gradually replacing the term 'chiropody'. Foot problems affect about three-quarters of the population and podiatrists provide specialist foot care and advice, working in the NHS in hospitals and health clinics and in their own private surgeries. They deal with: children's foot problems, sports injuries, foot deformities, foot care for the elderly and the care of patients with rheumatoid arthritis or diabetes.

☞ Three- or four-year full-time degree course at a university or college of higher education. A good base of GCSEs at grades A, B or C, including English, and two A-levels, including one science subject, are normally required.

✍ **Further information** Society of Chiropodists, 53 Welbeck Street, London W1M 7HE
Institute of Chiropodists, 91 Lord Street, Southport, Merseyside PR8 1SA
☞ School careers library classification JAT

Civil engineering
see **Engineering**

Civil Service

Some civil servants work directly for government ministers, researching and advising on the formulation of policy. The majority work in head or local offices applying this policy. Departments such as the Department of Employment, the Department for Education, the Home Office and the Foreign Office all employ civil servants at executive, administrative and clerical grades. There are also professional, scientific and technical posts in the Civil Service, such as those held by librarians, cartographers, meteorologists and air traffic controllers, which are dealt with under the relevant headings elsewhere in this Careers Guide. Civil Service departments are being separated from the main Civil Service and are being set up as independent agencies. They are carrying out their own recruitment and setting their own entry requirements. All branches of the Civil Service carry out their own recruitment at clerical and executive officer level now. The position is changing rapidly and up-to-date information should be obtained from your local JobCentre or careers office.

Administrative trainees (including equivalent posts in the Diplomatic Service) – the 'fast stream'

☞ A good base of GCSEs at grades A, B or C is required; an honours or postgraduate degree is essential as competition is very keen. (See GCSEs and higher education on page 132.)

Executive officer

☞ There are no longer any nationally applied requirements but agencies will normally be recruiting candidates with three GCSEs, including English, and two A-levels. Many successful candidates are graduates or hold BTEC Higher National awards.

Clerical posts

☞ There are no longer any nationally applied educational requirements and recruitment is carried out locally. Some agencies will require five GCSEs at grades A, B or C, including English, and for posts as clerical assistants two GCSEs at grades A, B or C, including English.

✍ **Further information** Recruitment and Assessment Services Agency, Alençon Link, Basingstoke, Hampshire RE21 1JB (fast stream only)

🎜 **Reading** *Working In* series: *Working in the Civil Service* published by and available from the Careers and Occupational Information Centre, price £2.65

☞ School careers library classification CAB

Clerical
see **Civil Service, Local government administration** *and* **Secretarial work**

Community work
see **Youth and community work**

Company secretaryship

A company secretary acts as a company's legal representative and ensures that it operates within the law. Company secretaries are responsible for keeping a register of shareholders and calling shareholders' meetings, paying dividends on shares and taking minutes at Board meetings. They may also advise the Board on financial and legal matters. In some companies the company secretary may also carry out personnel and other administrative functions.

☛ Three-year full-time or equivalent part-time course for the examinations of the Institute of Chartered Secretaries and Administrators (ICSA). The ICSA's Open Access policy means that anyone who is 17 years of age or over can study for the ICSA examinations on the Foundation Programme without previous academic qualifications.

☛ Entry after higher education: see GCSEs and higher education on page 132. Any degree will give exemption from the Foundation and the Pre-professional stages. BTEC Higher award holders will also gain exemptions. Note: The Institute's examinations are designed for general administrators as well as company secretaries.

✍ **Further information** Institute of Chartered Secretaries and Administrators, 16 Park Crescent, London W1N 4AH

▥ **Reading** First enquiry packs are available free from the Institute

☛ School careers library classification CAP

Computing work and information technology

Although most people will find some aspects of their working life affected by computers, computing personnel specialise and work solely in computing and information technology.

Data entry, transferring information by typing from paper to a form that the computer can 'read', is normally part of clerical or secretarial work (see Secretarial work).

☛ On-the-job training or computer-familiarity courses at further education colleges. Some GCSEs, not necessarily at grades A, B or C, are generally required.

Computer programmers write the code for the instructions (program) to operate the computer. The equipment is known as hardware and the programming side software.

☛ Part-time, day-release or evening classes for the City and Guilds Certificate in Basic Computer Programming. GCSE mathematics is often required. Some employers stipulate 18 as a minimum age.

☛ Part-time, sandwich, block-release and full-time courses for the BTEC National Certificate/Diploma in Computer Studies. Four GCSEs at grades A, B or C or a BTEC First Certificate/Diploma are required.

Systems analysts understand and interpret the way a business organisation manages its work, including the use of its computers. They advise on and design the computer system.

Software engineers work in teams to design and update software (large-scale programs) frequently constructed from existing 'library' programs.

☛ Two-year full-time or three-year sandwich courses for the BTEC Higher National Diploma in Computing, Software Engineering or Mathematics, Statistics and Computing. Three GCSEs at grades A, B or C, including mathematics, and one A-level or a BTEC National award

are required for entry. Part-time courses leading to the
BTEC Higher National Certificate in Computer Studies
have the same entry requirements as the Higher National
Diploma.

☛ Entry after higher education: see GCSEs and higher
education on page 132. Formerly graduates of all degree
subjects were recruited for computing but now most
successful candidates have taken degree courses with
some computer content. Degrees in computing require a
good base of GCSEs, including good grades in English
and mathematics, and at least two A-levels. Some colleges
require A-level mathematics.

✍ **Further information** British Computer Society,
PO Box 1454, Station Road, Swindon SN1 1TG
National Computing Centre, Bracken House, Charles
Street, Manchester M1 7BD

📶 **Reading** *Working In* series: *Computing* published by
and available from the Careers and Occupational
Information Centre, price £2.65
Computer Science Degree Course Guide published by
Hobsons Publishing PLC, price £4.99

☛ School careers library classification CAV

Consumer advice work
see **Trading standards administration**

Customs and Excise work

Customs and Excise officers are the civil servants who are
responsible for the collection of customs duties and the
prevention of the illegal import and export of prohibited
goods, such as drugs and firearms. This is only a small
proportion of their work, for they are responsible for the
collection of Value Added Tax (VAT) and excise duties on
oil, petrol, tobacco, wine and spirits.

Executive officer
☛ Three GCSEs at grades A, B or C, including English,

and two A-levels are required. All subjects are acceptable. Minimum age 17$^1/_2$. In practice many entrants are graduates or holders of BTEC Higher awards.

Administrative officer
(formerly clerical officer)
☛ Five GCSEs at grades A, B or C, including English, are required. All subjects are acceptable. Local recruitment.

Administrative assistant
(formerly clerical assistant)
Two GCSEs at grades A, B or C, including English, are required. Local recruitment.

✍ **Further information**
Recruitment and Assessment Services Agency, Alençon Link, Basingstoke, Hampshire RG21 1JB
Local Collector of Customs and Excise (address from the local telephone directory)

📖 **Reading** *Executive Opportunities in HM Customs and Excise* published by and available free from Personnel Division A2, HM Customs and Excise, 6th Floor Central, New King's Beam House, 22 Upper Ground, London SE1 9PJ

☛ School careers library classification CAB

Dairy farming
see **Farming and agricultural advisory work**

Dairy technology

Dairy technologists apply their scientific training to the collection, storage and processing of milk and the manufacture of a wide range of milk-based products, such as cheese, yogurts and ice-cream.

☛ Two-year full-time, three-year sandwich or part-time courses for the BTEC National Certificate/Diploma in

Science (Technology of Food) specialising in dairy technology. Four GCSEs at grades A, B or C, including mathematics and science, or a BTEC First Certificate/Diploma in Science are required. This can be followed by a BTEC Higher National Diploma in Science (Technology of Food). Alternative entry qualifications for the BTEC Higher National courses are one A-level in a science subject and GCSEs at grades A, B or C in English and a subject demonstrating numeracy.

☛ Entry after higher education: see GCSEs and higher education on page 132. Degrees in food science or technology require a good base of GCSEs at grades A, B or C, including double award science, followed by chemistry and two other science or mathematics subjects at A-level or a BTEC National Diploma in Science.

✍ **Further information** Dairy Trade Federation, 19 Cornwall Terrace, London NW1 4QP

▥ **Reading** *Food for your Future* and *The Dairy Industry Employment Directory* published by the National Dairy Council and available free from the Dairy Trade Federation

☛ School careers library classification SAC

Dancing

Dancers may work as stage performers of ballet and contemporary and modern dance, teach children and adults, or plan dance sequences (which is known as choreography).

☛ For diploma courses, GCSEs at grades A, B or C in English and mathematics are required. For degree courses, two A-levels as well as a good base of GCSEs are required. For the courses leading to recognised teacher status, the entrance requirements are the same as those of other teaching courses.

✍ **Further information** Council for Dance Education and Training (CDET), 5 Tavistock Place, London WC1H 9SS

▥ Reading CDET publishes a range of information leaflets covering various areas of dance training. These are available free if a large stamped addressed envelope is sent
☞ School careers library classification GAF

Data processing
see **Computing work and information technology**

Decorating
see **Building crafts** *and* **Art and design**

Dental hygiene work

Dental hygienists work under the direction of a dentist. They scale, clean and polish teeth, apply preventive materials which help reduce dental decay and give oral hygiene instruction.
☞ Full-time course lasting about one year for the Diploma in Dental Hygiene. Five GCSEs at grades A, B or C, including at least a single award science, are required. All candidates should normally have had two years' experience as a dental surgery assistant and preferably hold a nationally recognised certificate in dental surgery assisting. Minimum age 17.
✑ **Further information** General Dental Council, 37 Wimpole Street, London W1M 8DQ
British Dental Hygienists Association, 64 Wimpole Street, London W1M 8AL
▥ Reading *Dental Hygienist* published by and available free from the General Dental Council
☞ School careers library classification JAF

Dental surgery assisting

Dental surgery assistants help the dentist by preparing materials and equipment, assisting at the chairside, sterilising instruments, looking after patients and doing paperwork.

☛ One- or two-year full-time, day-release or evening course at dental hospitals and colleges of further education. There are no longer any academic entry requirements, age limits or experience requirements to take the National Certificate for Dental Surgery Assistants.

✍ **Further information** The Association of British Dental Surgery Assistants, 29 London Street, Fleetwood, Lancashire FY7 6JY

▥ **Reading** *Dental Surgery Assisting as a Career* published by and available free from the Association *Dental Surgery Assistant* published by and available free from the General Dental Council

☛ School careers library classification JAF

Dental technician work

Dental technicians construct and repair false teeth, crowns and the orthodontic appliances which are used for straightening teeth. Their work is initiated by a prescription from a dentist.

☛ Three-year full-time, four-year sandwich or five-year day-release course while working in a laboratory for the BTEC National Diploma in Science (Dental Technology). Four GCSEs at grades A, B or C, including mathematics and preferably double award science, or a BTEC First Certificate are required for entry.

✍ **Further information** The Training Officer, The Dental Laboratories Association, Chapel House, Noel Street, Nottingham NG7 6AS

Dental Technicians Standards and Training Advisory Board, 64 Wimpole Street, London W1M 8DQ

▥ **Reading** *The Dental Technician* published by and available from A E Morgan Publications Ltd, Stanley House, 9 West Street, Epsom, Surrey KT18 7RL

The Dental Technician published by and available free
from the Dental Technicians Standards and Training
Advisory Board
☛ School careers library classification JAF

Dental therapy work

Dental therapists, who used to be called dental auxiliaries,
work under the direction of a dentist in a hospital,
community dental service or school dental clinic. They do
simple fillings, extract milk teeth and scale and polish
teeth. They do not work for dentists in private practice.
☛ Two-year full-time course at the London Hospital
which also includes qualification as a dental hygienist.
Five GCSEs at grades A, B or C are required, preferably
including English and at least a single award science as
well as experience as a dental surgery assistant and the
National Certificate for Dental Surgery Assistants.
Minimum age 18. Only eight places are available each
year.
✍ **Further information** Dental Auxiliary School,
London Hospital Medical College, 36 New Road, London
E1 2AX
▥ **Reading** *Dental Therapist* published by and available
free from the General Dental Council, 37 Wimpole Street,
London W1M 8DQ
☛ School careers library classification JAF

Dentistry

Dentists conserve teeth by filling, crowning and bridge-
work and try to prevent dental disease. They take out
teeth and design false teeth to replace them. They correct
irregular teeth in children by using plates and braces: this
is called orthodontics.
☛ A degree in dentistry is essential and entry to a degree
course requires a good base of GCSEs at grades A, B or C
together with three A-levels, one of which generally has to

be chemistry with two others chosen from mathematics, physics and biological subjects. GCSEs at grades A, B or C in mathematics and double award science are recommended. Some longer courses are run for candidates who have arts or a mixture of arts and science A-levels. See GCSEs and higher education on page 132.

✍ **Further information** General Dental Council, 37 Wimpole Street, London W1M 8DQ

📖 **Reading** *Dentistry Degree Course Guide*, published by Hobsons Publishing PLC, price £4.99

☛ School careers library classification JAF

Design
see **Art and design**

Dietetics

Dietitians are trained specialists who apply the science of nutrition to everyday eating, by promoting good food habits in people of all ages. Many work in hospitals where they teach and advise patients on diet for certain diseases; others work in the community advising the elderly or school-children.

☛ Four-year degree course in nutrition (with State Registration in dietetics) or a four-year degree course in dietetics. These courses usually require a good base of GCSEs at grades A, B or C, including English and preferably double award science and mathematics. At least two A-levels in science preferably including chemistry are also required. Graduates who have studied human biochemistry and physiology to a suitable standard can take a two-year postgraduate diploma course. See GCSEs and higher education on page 132.

✍ **Further information** British Dietetic Association, 7th Floor, Elizabeth House, 22 Suffolk Street, Queensway, Birmingham B1 1LS

📖 **Reading** *How to Qualify as a Dietitian* published by

and available free from the British Dietetic Association;
please enclose a large stamped addressed envelope
☞ School careers library classification JAV

Diplomatic Service
see **Civil Service**

Dispensing assistant/pharmacy technician work

Dispensing assistants help pharmacists to make up
prescriptions; they work in hospitals and in chemists'
shops.
☞ Two-year part-time (day-release or evening) course
for the Society of Apothecaries' Pharmacy Technician's
Certificate. Three academic GCSEs at grades A, B or C,
preferably including at least a single award in science, are
required. Minimum age for taking the examination is 18.
There is discussion about the future of the Certificate
with the introduction of National Vocational
Qualifications. Latest information can be gained from the
Society.
☞ Three-year part-time course for the BTEC National
Certificate in Science (Pharmaceutical). Four GCSEs at
grades A, B or C, including mathematics and single award
science, or a BTEC First Certificate/Diploma are required
for entry.
✍ **Further information** The Society of Apothecaries of
London, Black Friars Lane, London EC4V 6EJ
☞ School careers library classification JAG

Dispensing optics

Dispensing opticians supply and fit glasses prescribed by a
specially qualified doctor or an optometrist (ophthalmic
optician). They do not test sight.

☛ Part-time (day-release) courses at colleges of further education or by correspondence course, for the examinations of the Association of British Dispensing Opticians together with three years' employment. Five GCSEs at grades A, B or C, including English or English literature and mathematics, are required. All subjects are acceptable.

☛ Two-year full-time course for the examination of the Association of British Dispensing Opticians plus a year's experience following the final examination. Five GCSEs at grades A, B or C, including English or English literature, mathematics or at least a single award science, are required. All subjects are acceptable.

✍ **Further information** Association of British Dispensing Opticians, 7 Hurlingham Business Park, Sullivan Road, London SW6 3DU

📖 **Reading** *A Career in Vision Care* published by and available free from the General Optical Council, 41 Harley Street, London W1N 2DJ

☛ School careers library classification JAL

Display work
see **Art and design**

Drama

Apart from acting, which is a very overcrowded profession, there are careers in stage production and stage management.

☛ Three-year full-time course in acting or stage management at a drama school. Academic qualifications are not as important as evidence of potential dramatic ability, although many drama students will have GCSEs and A-levels.

☛ Degree courses where drama is often combined with another subject. A good base of GCSEs at grades A, B or C is required with at least two A-levels. English is sometimes required at A-level. These are academic and are not stage training. Some colleges of higher education offer drama as part of a BEd course.

|||| **Reading** *Working In* series: *Performing Arts* published by and available from the Careers and Occupational Information Centre, price £2.95

☛ School careers library classification GAB

Dyeing

Dyeing is concerned with the production of coloured textile materials.

☛ Full-time or part-time college courses for a BTEC National Certificate/Diploma in Science (Textile Coloration). Four GCSEs at grades A, B or C, including mathematics and at least single award science, or a BTEC First Certificate/Diploma are required for entry. Successful students may subsequently take the BTEC Higher National Certificate/Diploma in Science (Textile Coloration) after a further two years. The Higher National courses can also be entered by candidates with three GCSEs, including mathematics, single award science and a subject testing command of English, and one A-level. Professional qualifications awarded by the Society of Dyers and Colourists – namely the Certificate in Coloration and the Associateship of the Society – may be taken after a further one year and two years respectively.

☛ Entry after higher education: see GCSEs and higher education on page 132. Several universities run degree courses in colour chemistry. A good base of GCSEs at grades A, B or C is required and A-levels preferably in chemistry, mathematics and physics. Some chemistry students are able to take either special papers in colour chemistry or a postgraduate course in colour chemistry after completing their degree course.

✍ **Further information** The Society of Dyers and Colourists, Perkin House, PO Box 244, 82 Grattan Road, Bradford BD1 2JB

📖 **Reading** *Careers in Colour* published by and available free from the Society of Dyers and Colourists
☞ School careers library classification QOB

Economics

Economists are social scientists who are concerned with questions such as the reasons for high unemployment, the balance of payments, the amount of public expenditure and the effect of taxation.
☞ A degree course is essential. A good base of GCSEs at grades A, B or C, including mathematics, and at least two A-levels are required. The A-levels may be in any subjects, although mathematics is often preferred. A-level economics is never required to enter a degree course. See GCSEs and higher education on page 132.
📖 **Reading** *Economics Degree Course Guide* published by Hobsons Publishing PLC, price £4.99
☞ School careers library classification QOK

Electrical engineering
see **Engineering**

Electronic and radio engineering
see **Engineering**

Engineering

Engineering covers an extremely wide field of careers. This section deals with the work of chartered engineers, incorporated engineers and engineering technicians. The next section deals with engineering craft work.

Aeronautical engineering
The aircraft industry can be split into 'airframes' and

'engines'. Designing airframes includes aerodynamics, structural design and the design of the systems within the aircraft. Aerodynamics covers the basic shape of the aircraft related to performance. Structural design has become more complex because of the introduction of new materials. 'Systems' covers the heating and ventilation systems within the aircraft, the radar and the flight control. The 'engines' side of the industry requires aeronautical engineers, particularly for the study of air flows inside the engines; many mechanical engineers also work on this side. In addition to doing design work, aeronautical engineers service and repair aircraft for airline operators and are employed by British Aerospace to develop and construct their communications and other satellites.

✍ **Further information** Royal Aeronautical Society, 4 Hamilton Place, London W1V 0BQ

☛ School careers library classification RAC

Chemical and biochemical engineering

Chemical engineering theory can be applied to a wide range of process industries because the processes can be split up into operations which are essentially the same. Thus, distillation occurs in whisky manufacture and oil refining and filtration is common to sewage treatment, drugs manufacture and the concentration of mineral ores. Chemical engineers study these processes and design, construct and operate the plant in which they take place. Computer control and design is a standard feature of chemical engineering and all courses include training in this field. Safety and environmental issues are high on the agenda of chemical engineers who can make a positive contribution in the design and running of plants.

✍ **Further information** The Institution of Chemical Engineers, 12 Gayfere Street, London SW1P 3HP

☛ School careers library classification RAG

Civil engineering

Civil engineers plan, design, construct and maintain

roads, railways, airports, bridges, tunnels, water supplies and reservoirs. The supply and distribution of energy is also an area of work for civil engineers who design and build North Sea oil platforms, pipelines and hydro-electric schemes.

Structural engineering is a specialised area of civil engineering. It is the science and art of designing and constructing structures such as bridges, the framework and foundations of large buildings, oil rigs, aircraft and space structures.

Many civil engineers work for local authorities where they are in charge of the building of roads and bridges and also concerned with street lighting, refuse collection and the control of pollution. Transportation planning, which deals with traffic management schemes such as one-way streets and the siting of roundabouts, traffic lights and car parks as well as the effective operation of public transport, overlaps with town and country planning. Civil engineers help developing countries with irrigation schemes, sanitation and transport which are essential to combat disease and malnutrition.

✍ **Further information** Civil Engineering Careers Service, 1–7 Great George Street, London SW1P 3AA Institution of Structural Engineers, 11 Upper Belgrave Street, London SW1X 8BH

☛ School careers library classification UN

Electrical and electronic engineering

Electrical engineers are responsible for generating electricity and then bringing it to heat and light buildings and providing a continuous source of power for equipment used in homes, schools, offices and hospitals. It is the electrical engineers who will work out new methods of producing electricity when our traditional resources no longer exist.

Electronic engineers work in the rapidly expanding field of communications. Microelectronic technology has enabled these engineers to develop highly sophisticated computers and information systems which are now being used in transport, business, industry and medicine. Computers control industrial processes and robots are now widely used in industrial production. Particularly important are the life-saving applications of micro-electronics in hospitals: heart–lung machines and kidney dialysers, etc.

✍ **Further information** Schools Education and Liaison Service, Institution of Electrical Engineers, Michael Faraday House, Six Hills Way, Stevenage, Hertfordshire SG1 2AY

☞ School careers library classification RAK and RAL

Energy engineering

Energy engineers apply their scientific knowledge to the preparation and burning of coal, gas, oil and nuclear fuel for heating, lighting and power. Some may work in fuel conservation, being concerned with the most efficient use of the Earth's dwindling supplies of fossil fuels.

Gas engineers mainly work for British Gas supplying gas to consumers in Great Britain. They also work for companies making gas appliances such as cookers, fires and boilers. Gas engineering covers both civil engineering – the provision of pipelines and gas holders – and chemical engineering, producing gas from coal or oil and the exploration for further gas supplies. Since the discovery and use of natural gas in the UK, the gas industry has expanded and there are more opportunities for gas engineers.

✍ **Further information** Institute of Energy, 18 Devonshire Street, London W1N 2AU
The Institution of Gas Engineers, 17 Grosvenor Crescent, London SW1X 7ES

☞ School careers library classification RAN

Maritime engineering

Marine engineers work on the design, construction,

operation and maintenance of ships' engines and systems. Many work in the Merchant Navy as engineer officers where they are responsible for the safe and efficient operation of the ship's engines and associated systems. **Naval architects** are not concerned with the engines that move the ship through the water, but with the design, construction, stability and performance of the ship's hull and various types of construction in the offshore industry.

Marine engineers and naval architects work in close co-operation on projects in offshore/subsea engineering and structural, mechanical, civil and electrical engineering with marine applications.

✍ **Further information** Institute of Marine Engineers, The Memorial Building, 76 Mark Lane, London EC3R 7JN Royal Institution of Naval Architects, 10 Upper Belgrave Street, London SW1X 8BQ

☞ School careers library classification RAV and ROF

Mechanical engineering

Mechanical engineering includes most technical activities in which moving parts are involved. Mechanical engineers work closely with engineers of other disciplines and work in design, manufacture, installation, operation and maintenance of machinery of all kinds. They work in fields as diverse as biomechanics, satellite systems, nuclear power, materials science and food technologies.

✍ **Further information** Schools Liaison Service, Institution of Mechanical Engineers, Northgate Avenue, Bury St Edmunds, Suffolk IP32 6BN

☞ School careers library classification RAX

Mining engineering

Mining engineers design and manage mining operations so they are profitable, safe and harm the environment as little as possible. There are specialist opportunities in ventilation, environmental engineering, rock mechanics, prospecting, mineral processing, mining surveying and drilling engineering. Most openings in the UK are with British Coal and a growing number of quarrying companies, but there are many opportunities abroad in metal mining.

✍ **Further information** Institution of Mining Engineers, Danum House, South Parade, Doncaster DN1 2DY

Institution of Mining and Metallurgy, 44 Portland Place, London W1N 4BR

☛ School careers library classification ROB

Education and training

Chartered Engineer (CEng) If you are planning from the outset to be a chartered engineer you should have a good base of GCSEs at grades A, B or C, including mathematics, double award science and preferably English, for later specialisation in sciences at A-level. Most accredited degree courses leading to chartered engineer status require A-levels in mathematics and physics; for courses in chemical engineering, A-levels in mathematics and chemistry are generally required. A good BTEC National Certificate/Diploma is an alternative entry qualification. You should take a full-time or sandwich degree course in engineering at a university or college of higher education that has been accredited by a professional engineering institution. Such a course exempts students from the examinations of the Engineering Council. Some engineering companies sponsor students on these courses.

In addition to the courses, you must undergo a two-year period of practical training and two years of professional responsibility. This will vary according to the institution you join but will not be less than four years in total. To be registered as a chartered engineer you must also have corporate membership of one of the institutions of the Chartered Engineer Section of the Board for Engineers Registration of the Engineering Council.

Incorporated Engineer (IEng) Two-year full-time or three-year sandwich or equivalent part-time accredited courses for the BTEC Higher National Diploma/ Certificate in Engineering for which the entry requirements are four GCSEs at grades A, B or C and two subjects, usually mathematics and physics, will have been studied to A-level and one of these passed at A-level. The most useful GCSE subjects would be English, mathematics, computer studies, technology and double award science. A BTEC National Certificate/Diploma with relevant units is an alternative entry qualification to BTEC Higher award courses. In addition to an academic course, for IEng you must have four years' relevant engineering experience, including two years' approved practical training. To be registered as an incorporated engineer you must also have membership of one of the institutions of the Incorporated Engineer Section of the Board for Engineers Registration of the Engineering Council.

Engineering Technician (EngTech) For entry to a two- or three-year BTEC National Certificate/Diploma programme four GCSEs at grades A, B or C or a BTEC First Certificate/Diploma in Engineering are required. In addition you must have three years' engineering experience including two years' approved practical training and are encouraged to become a member of one of the institutions of the Engineering Technician Section of the Board for Engineers Registration of the Engineering Council.

Engineering Council: Board for Engineers Registration

The Engineering Council, a Royal Chartered body set up in 1981 to promote the science and practice of engineering, has taken over the principal responsibility for the registration of engineers in collaboration with the individual professional institutions. The following are constituent members of the Board for Engineers Registration. It is important to note that a member institution may require qualifications that differ from, or are additional to, those called for by the Board and this should be checked with the particular institution concerned.

1 Chartered engineer entry
2 Incorporated engineer entry
3 Engineering technician entry

Association of Cost Engineers 1
Biological Engineering Society 1 (Affiliate), 2, 3
British Computer Society 1, 2
British Institute of Non-Destructive Testing 1
    (Affiliate), 2, 3
Chartered Institution of Building Services Engineers 1, 2, 3
Institute of Acoustics 1 (Affiliate), 2
Institute of British Foundrymen 1 (Affiliate), 2, 3
Institute of Energy 1, 2
Institute of Engineers and Technicians 2, 3
Institute of Highway Incorporated Engineers 2, 3
Institute of Hospital Engineering 1 (Affiliate), 2, 3
Institute of Marine Engineers 1, 2, 3
Institute of Materials 1, 2, 3
Institute of Measurement and Control 1, 2, 3
Institute of Physics 1 (Affiliate)
Institute of Plumbing 2, 3
Institute of Quality Assurance 2, 3
Institute of Road Transport Engineers 2, 3
Institution of Agricultural Engineers 1 (Affiliate), 2, 3
Institution of Chemical Engineers 1, 2
Institution of Civil Engineers 1, 2, 3
Institution of Electrical Engineers 1
Institution of Electronics and Electrical Incorporated
    Engineers 2, 3
Institution of Engineering Designers 1 (Affiliate), 2, 3
Institution of Gas Engineers 1, 2, 3

Institution of Incorporated Executive Engineers 2, 3
Institution of Lighting Engineers 1 (Affiliate), 2, 3
Institution of Mechanical and Incorporated Engineers 2, 3
Institution of Mechanical Engineers 1
Institution of Mining and Metallurgy 1, 2
Institution of Mining Electrical and Mining Mechanical
    Engineers 1 (Affiliate), 2, 3
Institution of Mining Engineers 1, 2, 3
Institution of Nuclear Engineers 1 (Affiliate), 2
Institution of Plant Engineers 1 (Affiliate), 2, 3
Institution of Structural Engineers 1, 2
Institution of Water and Environmental Management 1
    (Affiliate), 2, 3
Institution of Water Officers 2, 3
Institution of Works and Highways Management 2, 3
Minerals Engineering Society 1 (Affiliate), 2, 3
North East Coast Institution of Engineers and
    Shipbuilders 1 (Affiliate), 2, 3
Royal Aeronautical Society 1, 2, 3
Royal Institution of Naval Architects 1, 2, 3
Welding Institute 1 (Affiliate), 2, 3
✍ **Further information** Engineering Council,
10 Maltravers Street, London WC2R 3ER
Engineering Training Authority, Careers and Information
Services, Vector House, 41 Clarendon Road, Watford,
Hertfordshire WD1 1HS (for careers in manufacturing
industry)
Civil Engineering Careers Service, 1–7 Great George
Street, London SW1P 3AA
Women's Engineering Society, Department of Civil
Engineering, Imperial College of Science and Technology,
Imperial College Road, London SW7 2BU
Individual institutions
📖 **Reading** A range of free leaflets is published by and
available from the Engineering Training Authority and
the Civil Engineering Careers Service. Please specify the
level of career that interests you.

☞ School careers library classification R

Engineering crafts

Engineering craftsmen and women are skilled workers able to follow engineering drawings and instructions prepared by professional engineers. In manufacturing industry, where the majority of engineering craftspeople work, they can be divided into

(i) craft machinists who shape metal into components. Turners use lathes which rotate a workpiece from which metal is removed with a fixed cutting tool. Millers use milling machines which remove metal from a fixed workpiece. Toolmakers make a variety of tools such as jigs, fixtures and cutters which are used in the production process.

(ii) fitters and electricians. Fitters assemble machines in factories deciding on the order of the work needed to make sure the parts fit and work together. They also repair and maintain machines on the customers' premises – in factories as well as private houses. So a gas fitter, for example, will repair gas stoves, gas fires and central heating boilers, finding faults and correcting them. Electricians work on electrical installation, putting electrical systems into new buildings or replacing them in old buildings. They repair electrical equipment, including both ordinary household appliances and industrial machinery. Electronics servicing covers the repair of radio, TV and of other electronic equipment such as computers.

(iii) metal fabrication workers. Welders join or cut metal using oxyacetylene or other types of equipment. Sheet metal workers make complicated shaped items from thin metal sheets.

(iv) metal processors. A moulder reproduces the shape of a component in reverse form in a sand mould. Molten metal is poured into the completed mould to form a casting.

☛ Three- to four-year apprenticeship with a firm. The majority of craft trainees follow the training pattern recommended by the Engineering Training Authority (ENTRA). The first year is spent at training centres approved by ENTRA, the second and third years are spent in 'module training' either within the firm or at a centre which has specialist facilities. Trainees can in addition take City and Guilds or BTEC courses at local further education colleges. Some firms offer Youth Training (YT) Scheme courses. There are no formal entry requirements but most employers give preference to candidates with GCSEs at around grade E or higher in mathematics, science, computer studies and technological subjects.

An important engineering craft level career outside manufacturing industry is the motor mechanic who repairs all types of road vehicles. They usually specialise in light vehicles, such as cars and vans, or in heavy vehicles, eg lorries and buses, or motorbikes. In most garages mechanics do either repairs and servicing or bodywork, which can include panel beating, welding and spray painting.

☛ Day-release, block-release or evening courses at colleges of further education for City and Guilds certificates while working in a garage. There are no formal entry qualifications but employers may give preference to candidates with GCSEs at around grade E or higher in mathematics, science and technological subjects.

✍ **Further information** Engineering Training Authority, Careers and Information Service, Vector House, 41 Clarendon Road, Watford, Hertfordshire WD1 1HS (for careers in manufacturing industry)

▥ **Reading** Booklets published by and available free from the Engineering Training Authority Careers and Information Service

☛ School careers library classification: various under R

Environmental health

Environmental health officers work for local authorities
to ensure a healthy environment for us all. They inspect
housing, restaurants and shops where food is sold. They
monitor levels of air pollution and deal with complaints
about excessive noise. There are increasing opportunities
in the private sector.

☛ Four-year sandwich course leading to a degree in
environmental health. Three GCSEs at grades A, B or C,
including mathematics, English and at least a single award
science, and two A-levels, one of which must be a science
subject, are normally required. Some part-time degree
courses are available. See GCSEs and higher education on
page 132.

✍ **Further information** Institution of Environmental
Health Officers, Chadwick House, Rushworth Street,
London SE1 0QT

▥ **Reading** *EHO: The Role of the Environmental Health
Officer* and *A Career in Environmental Health* both
available free from the Institution

☛ School careers library classification COP

Estate agency, auctioneering and valuation

Estate agents act for people wishing to sell property – not
only houses but also farms, factories, shops and offices.
They arrange mortgages and also manage property on
behalf of landlords – collecting rents and arranging for
repairs to be done. Auctioneers sell property as well as
animals, furniture and second-hand goods. Valuers assess
the value of all types of property for rates, tax, probate
and insurance purposes. They work in local authorities,
the Inland Revenue and for estate agents and auctioneers.
Estate agents and auctioneers do not have to be professionally

qualified but many have one of the following qualifications.

☞ Part-time study for the examinations of the Architects' and Surveyors' Institute using the syllabus of the Confederation of Construction Professions; details from the Institute.

☞ Three-year full-time course, or an equivalent part-time or correspondence course, for the examinations of the Incorporated Society of Valuers and Auctioneers. Five GCSEs at grades A, B or C, including English and mathematics, or four GCSEs at grades A, B or C and one A-level, including English and mathematics at either level, are required for entry.

☞ Three- to four-year part-time course for the examinations of the Institute of Revenues, Rating and Valuation. Two A-levels and two GCSEs at grades A, B or C or one A-level and four GCSEs at grades A, B or C, including English and mathematics, are required. All GCSE and A-level subjects are acceptable.

☞ Part-time study for the examinations of the Incorporated Association of Architects and Surveyors. Three GCSEs at grades A, B or C and two A-levels are required. Mathematics, science and a subject requiring the use of descriptive English must be included at either level.

☞ Three-year full-time or four-year sandwich course for a recognised degree in estate management or building surveying. Three GCSEs at grades A, B or C and two A-levels are required. English and mathematics must be passed at either level. These degree courses give various exemptions from the examinations of the professional bodies: details from the individual professional bodies.

☞ Full-time or part-time college courses for a BTEC National Certificate/Diploma in Land Use (Estate Management). Four GCSEs at grades A, B or C, preferably including English and mathematics, or a BTEC First Certificate/Diploma are required for entry. A BTEC National course can be followed by a degree course

(above), professional qualifications or a BTEC Higher
National Certificate/Diploma in Estate Management.
Alternative entry requirements to HND are four GCSEs at
grades A, B or C, including English and mathematics, and
one A-level.

✍ **Further information** Incorporated Society of Valuers
and Auctioneers, 3 Cadogan Gate, London SW1X 0AS
Institute of Revenues, Rating and Valuation, 41 Doughty
Street, London WC1N 2LF
Architects' and Surveyors' Institute, 15 St Mary Street,
Chippenham, Wiltshire SN15 3JN
The Royal Institution of Chartered Surveyors, Surveyor
Court, Westwood Way, Coventry CV4 8JE

📖 **Reading** *Making Land, Property and Construction
Work* published by and available free from the Royal
Institution of Chartered Surveyors
Booklets published by and available free from the
Incorporated Society of Valuers and Auctioneers

☛ School careers library classification UM

Exporting

Exporters work in the marketing departments of large
companies, in import/export agencies and in confirming
houses. They obtain orders from overseas for British goods,
undertake the necessary documentation and arrange for
the goods to be shipped or air freighted. Some large
British companies maintain subsidiary companies abroad.

☛ Part-time study for the examinations of the Institute
of Export. Four GCSEs at grades A, B or C are required,
including English. Many employers prefer mathematics,
geography and a modern foreign language at GCSE. The
following subjects are not acceptable: art, child
development, drama and music. For those with no
academic qualifications, the Institute of Export's
Certificate in Export Office Practice is available at some
colleges. Minimum age 18.

☞ One-year day-release or evening course for the Advanced Certificate in Overseas Trade/Professional Examination Part I. Four GCSEs at grades A, B or C, including English, and one A-level are required. Minimum age 18. This course is also accepted as part of the qualification of the Institute of Freight Forwarders. The Chartered Institute of Marketing may give exemptions from their Certificate and Diploma examinations to successful candidates. Students can follow this with study for the Professional Part II/Diploma in Export Management.

☞ Two-year full-time, sandwich or three-year part-time course for the BTEC Higher National Diploma. At some colleges it is possible to take options in marketing. Three GCSEs at grades A, B or C and one A-level or a BTEC National Certificate or Diploma are required for entry.

☞ Three-year full-time or four-year sandwich course for a degree in business studies. Three GCSEs at grades A, B or C (many colleges require English and mathematics) and two A-levels are required. Some courses have options in international marketing. It is also possible at some universities to take degree courses in international marketing, usually as part of a modular programme. See GCSEs and higher education on page 132 about entry to higher education. Postgraduate courses in exporting are also available.

✍ **Further information** Institute of Export, 64 Clifton Street, London EC2A 4HB

▥ **Reading** *Working as a Professional Exporter* published by and available free from the Institute of Export

☞ School careers library classification OM

Farming and agricultural advisory work

Farming covers a wide variety of work and offers jobs for people at all levels of educational attainment. There are mixed farms – those with crops and livestock – but over the last few years there has been a tendency for farms to specialise in dairy cows, beef cattle, pigs, sheep, poultry or cereals. For agricultural advisory work or research a degree is usually required. Growing vegetables and fruit in market gardens is dealt with under Horticulture. All the courses below degree level will be replaced by National Vocational Qualifications (NVQs) over the next few years. Degree courses will eventually be linked with the NVQ system.

☛ Most 16 and 17 year-old school-leavers enter the industry through Youth Training (YT) Schemes which are most commonly managed by local agricultural colleges and departments. The one- or two-year schemes offer planned work experience on farms and vocational education and training through day and block release courses which will, in the future, lead to National Vocational Qualifications (NVQs) at Levels 1 and 2. There are no specific educational requirements but preference may be given to candidates who have some GCSEs at grade E and above.

☛ One-year full-time course for the National Certificate in General Agriculture, Dairy Farming or Poultry Husbandry. No formal entry qualifications are necessary but GCSEs at grade E or above in English, mathematics and at least a single award science would be helpful. At least one year's practical experience is essential. Students who achieve a high standard in the National Certificate can follow it with a one-year supplementary course for either the Advanced National Certificate in Agriculture or the National Certificate in Farm Management.

☛ Three-year sandwich course for the BTEC National Diploma in Agriculture. The second year is spent working on a farm. Four GCSEs at grades A, B or C, including double award science and one testing command of English, are required. On the course students can specialise in arable farming, livestock production, farm mechanisation or dairy farming. There is a separate two-year sandwich course in poultry husbandry. It is also possible to enter these courses with a good National Certificate.

☛ Three-year sandwich course for the BTEC Higher National Diploma in Agriculture. Four GCSEs, including a subject testing command of English and two distinct mathematics/science subjects, and one A-level normally in a science subject and another subject studied to A-level are required. Candidates may also enter with BTEC National Diplomas in Science or Agriculture.

☛ Three-year degree course in agriculture for which a good base of GCSEs at grades A, B or C, including mathematics and double award science, for later specialisation in A-level science subjects is required. See GCSEs and higher education on page 132 about entry to higher education.

✍ **Further information** Careers, Education and Training for Agriculture and the Countryside, 10 Northgate Street, Warwick CV34 4SR

National Examinations Board for Agriculture, Horticulture and Allied Industries, 46 Britannia Street, London WC1X 9RG

Business and Technology Education Council, Central House, Upper Woburn Place, London WC1H 0HH

▥ **Reading** *Agricultural Sciences Degree Course Guide* published for CRAC by Hobsons Publishing PLC, price £4.99

Directory of Courses in Land Based Industries published annually by ACER (East Anglia), Merlin Place, Milton Road, Cambridge CB4 4DP

Factsheets on courses in agriculture and related subjects
published by and available free from the Business and
Technology Education Council
Working In series: *Agriculture and Horticulture* published
by and available from the Careers and Occupational
Information Centre, price £2.35
☞ School careers library classification WAB

Fashion – clothing production

Most clothes are mass produced in factories. A team of
skilled clothing-production workers use mass-production
techniques to translate the design into a finished garment.

Cutters use an electric knife (sometimes computerised
cutting machinery) to cut out the separate pieces which
make up each garment. Sewing machinists put the
garment together often using a specialised machine for
each process. Pressers use a mechanical press or a hand
iron on the garments at stages in the production process
and when the garment has been completed. Examiners
inspect the garments at various stages to make sure faults
are spotted and repaired. There are also management and
technician level posts concerned with engineering, design
(see Art and design), production planning and financial
planning and control.

☞ For cutters, sewing machinists, pressers and
examiners: on-the-job training sometimes with day
release to attend courses at colleges of further education.
Many of these courses lead to City and Guilds Certificates.
No formal educational qualifications are required but some
employers give preference to candidates with GCSEs at grade
E or above. Many school-leavers now enter the
industry through Youth Training (YT). National Council for
Vocational Qualifications (NCVQ) certificates are being
introduced at Levels 1 and 2 covering various skills and
competencies.

Management and technician careers

☛ Two-year full-time course for the BTEC Higher National Diploma in Clothing for which either four GCSEs at grades A, B or C and one A-level or a BTEC National Diploma in Clothing are required.

☛ Four-year sandwich course for the examinations of the Clothing and Footwear Institute (CFI International). Five GCSEs at grades A, B or C, including English and either mathematics or science, and one A-level are required. All GCSE and A-level subjects are acceptable. After successful completion of the examinations and two years' experience in the clothing industry candidates qualify for the associateship of the Clothing and Footwear Institute (CFI International) which is degree equivalent.

☛ Four-year sandwich course leading to a degree in clothing studies. A good base of GCSEs at grades A, B or C, including English and mathematics, and two A-levels are required. See GCSEs and higher education on page 132 about entry to higher education.

✍ **Further information** Clothing and Footwear Institute (CFI International), Butlers Wharf Business Centre, Suite 105, 45 Curlew Street, London SE1 2ND
Careers Information Service, Clothing and Allied Products Industrial Training Board (CAPITB PLC), 80 Richardshaw Lane, Pudsey, Leeds LS28 6BN

▥ **Reading** *Working In* series: *Fashion* published by and available from the Careers and Occupational Information Centre, price £2.65

☛ School careers library classification EJ/SAH

Film and video production

Films and videos are made by a team composed of a camera operator, a sound recordist and a lighting specialist. A film editor then takes the film and cuts down the amount of footage shot. The director supervises the whole process. Depending on the size of the production the team may be composed of two or three people or over 30. Animated films (cartoons) are also produced by a team who, in addition to the work of an ordinary film, draw all the pictures. The British film industry is very small and outside the television companies there are few opportunities. For entry to all courses it is important to show an amateur interest in film- and video-making.

☛ Three-year full-time course for a degree in art and design specialising in film production. A minimum of five GCSEs at grades A, B or C and either two A-levels or the completion of a foundation course in art and design are required.

☛ Three-year full-time course for a degree in film and photography. A good base of GCSEs at grades A, B or C, including English and science, and at least two A-levels are required.

☛ A range of other courses is available. Entry qualifications vary from a good general education to a degree or comparable qualification.

☛ On-the-job training lasting about a year for BBC camera operators, sound operators or assistant film editors. Candidates should have at least GCSE grades A, B or C standard in a range of subjects and have an informed knowledge of the principles of cinematography and a lively interest in films and film-making. There are many candidates for every vacancy, so in practice much higher qualifications are required. Successful candidates usually have degrees or experience in film-making.

✍ **Further information** British Film Institute, 21 Stephen Street, London W1P 1PL

📖 **Reading** *Film and Television Training* published by and available from the Institute, price £4.25 including postage

Studying Film and Television published by and available from the Institute, price £4.25 including postage (when both books ordered together, £7.00 including postage)

☛ School careers library classification GAL

Fine art
see **Art and design**

Fire-fighting

Fire-fighters not only fight fires and save lives, they deal with all types of emergencies, such as road accidents and spillage of dangerous chemicals. They also inspect buildings to make sure that they comply with the fire prevention rules and instruct members of the public in fire-fighting techniques.

☛ Most brigades do not have formal entry qualifications but candidates with GCSEs at grade E or above in English, mathematics and double award science are most likely to satisfactorily complete the entrance tests. These consist of a series of ability range tests, assembled at national level, specifically for potential recruits to the fire service, together with interviews and, in some brigades, numeracy and literacy tests. Candidates must have good eyesight and pass a vigorous medical examination as fire-fighters have to be physically fit and agile. The minimum age is 18, although some brigades have a junior recruitment scheme with entry at 16. All candidates who are selected must successfully complete a 12-week basic course which is usually residential. Promotion is from within the service and only for those members who have passed the written and practical examinations.

✍ **Further information** Fire brigade headquarters (the address will be in the local telephone directory)

📖 **Reading** *And We Also Fight Fires – A Career in the Fire Service* published by and available free from the Home Office (Fire Department), Queen Anne's Gate, London SW1H 9AT and local fire brigade headquarters

Working In series: *The Emergency Services* published by and available from the Careers and Occupational Information Centre, price £2.50

☛ School careers library classification MAF

Floristry
see **Retail and wholesale distribution**

Food science and technology

Food scientists examine the chemistry and biology of foods from raw materials through processing to the final product. Food technologists use food science and other technological know-how to turn raw materials into finished products for the consumer.

☛ Two-year full-time or three-year sandwich course for the BTEC National Certificate/Diploma in Science (Technology of Food). Normally four GCSEs at grades A, B or C, including double award science and preferably English, or a BTEC First Certificate/Diploma are required for entry.

☛ Two-year full-time or three-year sandwich courses for the BTEC Higher National Diploma in Science (Technology of Food). One A-level in a science subject, GCSEs at grades A, B or C in English and a subject demonstrating numeracy or a BTEC National Certificate or Diploma in the technology of food or in science with appropriate units are required.

☛ A good base of GCSEs at grades A, B or C and at least two science A-levels are required for a degree in food science and technology. Chemistry A-level is normally essential. Graduates with science degrees can take postgraduate courses in food science. See GCSEs and higher education on page 132.

✍ **Further information** Institute of Food Science and Technology, 5 Cambridge Court, 210 Shepherd's Bush Road, London W6 7NL

Food Manufacturers' Council for Industrial Training, 6 Catherine Street, London WC2B 5JJ

▥ **Reading** *Careers in Food Science and Technology* and
*Where to Study for a Career in Food Science and
Technology* published by and single copies available free
from the Institute. Please enclose an A4 stamped
addressed envelope
☛ School careers library classification QON/SAB

Forestry

Forestry work is concerned with managing forests and
includes planting, tending, felling and the preparation
and marketing of timber. About half the people in
forestry work are employed by the Forestry Commission;
the remainder work for commercial forestry farms, large
forest estates and local authorities.

☛ Most 16 and 17 year-old school-leavers enter the
industry through Youth Training (YT) which is either
managed by local agricultural colleges or other approved
training organisations. The one- and two-year schemes
offer planned work experience and education through
day- and block-release courses leading to National
Vocational Qualifications at Levels 1 and 2. This training
leads to posts as forest workers. No formal educational
qualifications are required but employers may give
preference to candidates with some GCSEs at grade E or
above.

☛ Three-year sandwich course for the BTEC National
Diploma in Forestry. Four GCSEs at grades A, B or C are
required, including English, mathematics and at least a
single award science, or a BTEC First Diploma in Land
Based Industries (Forestry). Applicants must be at least 18
and have a minimum of one year's practical experience
before going to college. The BTEC National Diploma can
be followed by the Higher National Diploma course.
Applicants can also enter the HND course with four
GCSEs, including English, mathematics and at least single
award science, and one A-level in an appropriate subject.

☛ Degree course in forestry. A good base of GCSEs at grades A, B or C is required for specialisation in science subjects at A-level. See GCSEs and higher education on page 132.

✍ **Further information** Forestry Commission, Personnel Branch, 231 Corstorphine Road, Edinburgh EH12 7AT (about careers)

📖 **Reading** *Careers in Forestry* published by and available free from the Commission

Also see the addresses and publications listed under Farming and agricultural advisory work

☛ School careers library classification WAF

Fuel technology
see **Engineering – energy engineering**

Funeral work and work in cemeteries and graveyards

Funeral directors make funeral arrangements and embalmers prepare bodies for burial or cremation. Cemetery and graveyard workers administer cremations and burials and the upkeep of the premises and grounds.

☛ Part-time study for the Diploma in Funeral Directing. Twelve months' practical experience is needed before being able to sit the examinations. Part-time study for the examinations of the National Examinations Board of Embalmers or the Institute of Burial and Cremation Administration. For all these examinations GCSEs at grades A, B or C in English and mathematics exempt candidates from the preliminary examination.

✍ **Further information** National Association of Funeral Directors, 618 Warwick Road, Solihull, West Midlands B91 1AA

British Institute of Embalmers, Anubis House, 21c Station Road, Knowle, Solihull, West Midlands B93 0HL

Institute of Burial and Cremation Administration, The
Gatehouse, Kew Meadow Path, Richmond, Surrey TW9 4EN
National Examinations Board of Embalmers, Huxley
House, William Street, Redditch, Worcestershire B97 4AJ
☞ School careers library classification IP

Furniture design
see **Art and design**

Gardening
see **Horticulture**

Gas engineering
see **Engineering**

General practitioner
see **Medicine and surgery**

Geology

Geologists study the formation and structure of the
materials that make up the earth. This is a small
profession and some geologists do pure research –
research with no end in view except for increasing man's
knowledge of the world. Others work, often abroad, for
oil and mining companies that are looking to new sources
of minerals or as engineering geologists with civil
engineering firms.
☞ Three-year degree course in geology. A good base of
GCSEs at grades A, B or C for specialisation in science
A-levels is required. Three A-levels chosen from geology,
physics, chemistry, biological subjects, geography and
mathematical subjects are recommended for sixth-form
study. Subjects not held at A-level should generally
be held at GCSE, except for geology which is never
formally required for entry to a geology degree course.

✍ **Further information** British Geological Survey,
Keyworth, Nottingham NG12 5GG
Institution of Geologists, Geological Society Apartments,
Burlington House, Piccadilly, London W1V 9HG
▥ **Reading** *Careers in the Geological Sciences* published
by and available free from the British Geological Survey
Geology the Science: Geology the Profession published by
and available free from both the Institution and the
British Geological Survey
Geology and Environmental Sciences Degree Course Guide
published for CRAC by Hobsons Publishing PLC, price
£4.99
☛ School careers library classification QOL

Graphic design
see **Art and design**

Graphic reproduction
see **Printing – printing crafts**

Hairdressing
Hairdressers cut, shampoo, set, colour and perm hair.
Sometimes this career is combined with beauty therapy.
☛ Two-year full-time course at colleges of further
education, leading to National Vocational Qualification
(NVQ) Level 2. There are no formal entry requirements
but many colleges give preference to candidates with
some GCSEs at grade E or above, preferably in English,
mathematics and science.
☛ Two-year day-release course at colleges of further
education while working in a hairdresser's salon as an
apprentice. Many students enter hairdressing through
Youth Training (YT). Entry requirements as above.
✍ **Further information** The Guild of Hairdressers,
24 Woodbridge Road, Guildford, Surrey GU1 1DY (please
enclose a stamped addressed envelope)

Hairdressing Training Board, 3 Chequer Road, Doncaster, Yorkshire DN1 2AA

📖 **Reading** *Working In* series: *Hairdressing and Beauty* published by and available from the Careers and Occupational Information Centre, price £2.95

☛ School careers library classification IL

Health services management

Health services managers are non-medical staff who run hospitals, primary care and community health services.

☛ Day-release, evening or correspondence course, supported by activities arranged by regional education committees, for the examinations of the Institute of Health Services Management. Candidates must be working in health service units. Three GCSEs at grades A, B or C and two A-levels are required, including English and mathematics or another 'quantitative' science subject. The following subjects are not acceptable: drama, music, photography and textiles.

☛ Various training schemes run by regional health authorities for candidates with relevant qualifications, for example, BTEC National Certificates and Diplomas in Public Administration, accountancy qualifications, etc.

☛ A degree in any subject followed by study programmes leading to the examinations of the Institute of Health Services Management. See GCSEs and higher education on page 132.

✍ **Further information** Institute of Health Services Management, 75 Portland Place, London W1N 4AN

☛ School careers library classification CAL

Health visiting

Health visitors are nurses who work in the community to prevent disease. Their work is with people in all age groups but they concentrate particularly on young children and the old. They visit all mothers with children under five and advise on feeding and other aspects of care. They do not nurse the sick.

☛ One-year full-time course leading to the Health Visitor's Certificate for registered general nurses. Five GCSEs at grades A, B or C or an education entrance test are required. Some training schools may demand specific GCSE subjects and/or A-levels.

☛ Three- or four-year full-time degree course in nursing. A good base of GCSEs at grades A, B or C and at least two A-levels are required. Some universities and colleges specify science A-levels; colleges which do not require science A-levels will require double award science at GCSE. Some degree courses include options leading to the health visitor registration award. If there are no such options the degree course should be followed by a postgraduate course.

✍ **Further information** English National Board for Nursing, Midwifery and Health Visiting, Careers Service, PO Box 356, Sheffield s8 0sj

▥ **Reading** *Nursing in the Community (HSC 5)* published by the Department of Health and available free from Health Service Careers, PO Box 204, London se5 7es

☛ School careers library classification JAD

Home economics

The home economist is a professional adviser on food, nutrition, textiles, clothing, home management and design, household services and research related to the home and the community.

☛ Two-year full-time course for the City and Guilds Certificate in Home Economics for Family and Community Care No. 794. The course is designed for those who wish to choose employment in which home economics skills are relevant to working with people: with children, the elderly and the mentally and physically disabled. There are no specific educational requirements but for entry the colleges may give preference to candidates with some GCSEs at grade E or above. Certificate holders can become affiliates of the Institute of Home Economics.

☛ Full-time and part-time courses for the BTEC National Diploma/Certificate in Home Economics. Four GCSEs at grades A, B or C, a BTEC First Certificate/ Diploma or the City and Guilds Certificate in Home Economics are required for entry.

☛ Two-year full-time course for the BTEC Higher National Diploma in Home Economics. Four GCSEs at grades A, B or C, including English and a science, and one A-level, another subject having been studied to A-level, are required.

☛ Degree in home economics, food science or nutrition at a university or college of higher education. A good base of GCSEs at grades A, B or C and two A-levels are required. Science and home economics subjects are sometimes required at A-level or at GCSE. If you are intending to become a professional home economist after taking the degree course, you should check with the Institute that the course has the required content of home economics. See GCSEs and higher education on page 132.

✍ **Further information** Institute of Home Economics, Aldwych House, 71–91 Aldwych, London WC2B 4HN

▥ **Reading** *Careers in Home Economics* published by and available free from the Institute

☛ School careers library classification ID

Horses, work with

Grooms work in stables caring for the horses, riding instructors teach children and adults to ride; many people do both.

☛ 18- to 24-month part-time or full-time course leading to the examinations Horse Knowledge and Riding Stage

III and Preliminary Teaching Test of the British Horse
Society. Four GCSEs at grades A, B or C, including
English, are required in order to take the test under the
age of 17. All GCSE subjects are acceptable. No GCSEs are
required if the test is taken over the age of 18.

☛ Full-time college courses for the BTEC National
Diploma in Horse Management and similar awards. Four
GCSEs at grades A, B or C are required for entry.
Some 16 and 17 year-old leavers enter training through
Youth Training (YT). There are no formal entry
requirements.

✍ **Further information** British Horse Society, British
Equestrian Centre, Stoneleigh, Kenilworth, Warwickshire
CV8 2LR

📖 **Reading** *Working with Horses* published by and
available from the British Horse Society
Working In series: *Animals – Work With* published by and
available from the Careers and Occupational Information
Centre, price £2.65

☛ School careers library classification WAM

Horticulture

There are two main types of horticulture: commercial
horticulture, which is growing fruit, vegetables, cut
flowers and plants for sale, and amenity horticulture,
which is work in parks and gardens and the maintenance
of sports grounds and golf courses.

☛ Most 16 and 17 year-old school-leavers enter the
industry through Youth Training (YT) schemes which are
managed either by local agricultural and horticultural
colleges or by other approved training organisations. The
one- and two-year schemes offer planned work
experience on horticultural holdings and vocational
education and training through day- and block-release
courses which generally lead to National Vocational
Qualifications at Levels 1 and 2 in either Commercial or

Amenity Horticulture. There are no specific entry requirements but preference may be given to candidates who have some GCSEs at grade E or above.

☛ One-year full-time course for the National Certificate in Horticulture (Amenity or Commercial). No formal entry qualifications are necessary but GCSEs at grade E or above in English, mathematics and science are desirable. The minimum age is 17 and one year's practical experience is required; this may be a full-time introductory course in horticulture or a YT programme which includes eight months' practical experience. This National Certificate course can be followed by a supplementary one-year full-time course for the Advanced National Certificate in Horticulture or a BTEC National Diploma.

☛ Three-year sandwich course for the BTEC National Diploma in Commercial or Amenity Horticulture or in specialised sections of these subjects. Four GCSEs at grades A, B or C, including a subject testing command of English and either mathematics and single award science or double award science, are required. Minimum age is 17 (some colleges may require 18 minimum) and at least one year's practical experience is also required.

☛ Part-time study to help those employed in full-time practical horticulture who are taking the 'Master of Horticulture' examinations administered by the Royal Horticultural Society. Applicants are expected to have two A-levels including one science subject or their equivalent as the examinations are at a level equivalent to a university degree. At least three years' practical experience is required.

☛ Three-year sandwich course for the BTEC Higher National Diploma in Horticulture. Four GCSEs at grades A, B or C, including a subject testing command of English and two distinct mathematics/science subjects, one A-level and another subject studied at A-level are required. The A-level pass must be one of the following:

biology, botany, chemistry, computer studies, economics, engineering science, environmental studies, geography, geology, human biology, mathematics (any), physical science, physics, physics-with-chemistry, zoology. Candidates may also enter with BTEC National Diplomas in Science, Agriculture or Horticulture.

☞ Three- or four-year degree course in horticulture. A good base of GCSEs at grades A, B or C with further specialisation in A-level science subjects is required. Chemistry and a biological subject are the preferred A-level subjects. See GCSEs and higher education on page 132.

✍ **Further information** The Senior Scientist, Royal Horticultural Society, RHS Garden, Wisley, Woking, Surrey GU23 6QB

Institute of Horticulture, PO Box 313, 80 Vincent Square, London SW1P 2PE

The Local Government Management Board, Arndale House, Arndale Centre, Luton, Bedfordshire LU1 2TS (Training Scheme)

📖 **Reading** *Come into Horticulture* and an information sheet on courses published by and available free from the Institute of Horticulture (please enclose a stamped addressed envelope)

Please see the addresses and publications listed under Farming and agricultural advisory work

☞ School careers library classification WAD

Hotels
see **Catering, including hotel and institutional management**

Housing management

Housing managers work for housing organisations including local authorities, housing charities and trusts. They are involved in allocation, maintaining and planning rented accommodation. They must know about the structure of buildings, landlord and tenant law, and planning.

☛ Three-year part-time programme for the BTEC National Certificate in Housing Studies for which four GCSEs at grades A, B or C are required. This can be followed by the Higher National Certificate in Housing Studies which can also be entered with candidates holding one A-level. There are distance learning versions of the BTEC National and Higher National Certificate from the NALGO Correspondence Institute. Students can then take the Professional Diploma in Housing. This route takes about six years to become professionally qualified.

☛ Four-year sandwich or three-year full-time degree course in housing which is recognised by the Institute. A good base of GCSEs and at least two A-levels are required for entry. It is also possible to take these degree courses part-time.

☛ Degree in any subject followed by a one-year postgraduate course or three-year day-release courses for the Graduate Foundation Course and the Professional Diploma in Housing. See GCSEs and higher education on page 132.

✍ **Further information** Chartered Institute of Housing, Octavia House, Westwood Business Park, Westwood Way, Coventry, West Midlands CV4 8JP

▥ **Reading** *A Career in Housing* and a *Guide to Professional Qualification* published by and available free from the Institute

☛ School careers library classification UM

Industrial design
see **Art and design**

Information science

Information scientists (also called information officers)

collect and organise information about their organisation's work. They are involved in the whole process of information handling including abstracting, report writing, literature searches and information retrieval. The use of computers is an integral part of modern practice. There can be considerable overlap between the work done by information scientists and librarians, see page 247.

☛ A degree course in information science (very few available). A good base of GCSEs at grades A, B or C, including mathematics, science and a foreign language, and two A-levels are required.

☛ A degree in any subject, but preference is often given to candidates with degrees in scientific or technological subjects, followed by a postgraduate course in information science or an allied subject. See GCSEs and higher education on page 132.

☛ Both the Institute of Information Scientists and the Library Association accredit several degree and postgraduate courses in common for entry to professional membership. Employers will accept graduates from these courses for appointment to professional posts across the spectrum of library and information science.

✍ **Further information** Institute of Information Scientists, 44 Museum Street, London WC1A 1LY
The Education Department, The Library Association, 7 Ridgmount Street, London WC1E 7AE

▥ **Reading** *A Career in Information Science* published by and available free from the Institute
Various careers leaflets published by and available from the Library Association

☛ School careers library classification FAF

Institutional management
see **Catering, including hotel and institutional management**

Insurance

Insurance is a means by which many people pay small sums into a common fund, and then if some misfortune occurs such as an accident they can be compensated for their loss. Brokers act as intermediaries between the insurance companies and people wanting insurance. Most insurance companies have separate departments covering marine, aviation, motor, life, property and accident.

☛ Three- or four-year part-time courses for the Institute's Associateship examination followed by about two years' part-time study for the Institute's Fellowship examination. Three A-levels are required or two A-levels and two GCSEs at grades A, B or C, provided that one subject is English and that one of the A-levels is from the following list: English, natural sciences, economics, public and economic affairs, British Constitution, surveying, accounting (or principles of accounts), sociology, general principles of English law, business studies, general studies, religious knowledge. There is a special scheme for entrants over 20: details from the Institute.

☛ Full-time or part-time college courses for the BTEC National Certificate/Diploma in Business and Finance for which four GCSEs at grades A, B or C, including English and preferably mathematics, or a BTEC First Certificate are required for entry. This should be followed by study for the Institute's Associateship and Fellowship examinations.

☛ A degree or BTEC Higher National Diploma in any subject followed by study for the Institute's examinations. Candidates with certain degrees, for example business studies, may gain subject-for-subject exemptions.

✍ **Further information** Chartered Insurance Institute, Careers Department, 31 Hillcrest Road, South Woodford, London E18 2JP

The British Insurance and Investment Brokers' Association, BIIBA House, 14 Bevis Marks, London EC3A 7NT

IIII Reading Booklets published by and available free from the Chartered Insurance Institute

☛ School careers library classification NAG

Interior decoration and design
see **Art and design**

Interpreting
see **Language work**

ewellery
see **Retail and wholesale distribution** *and* **Art and design**

Journalism

Journalists work on provincial and national newspapers and magazines. They work as reporters, as feature writers producing articles on special topics and as specialists in areas such as sport or finance. Competition is extremely keen and successful entrants not only have the necessary academic qualifications but often show an interest in journalism by having written articles for school or college magazines and newspapers.

☛ A period of probation is usually followed by a training contract on a regional or local newspaper. The qualification period for taking the test is two years. During the qualification period trainees attend college and are expected to pass examinations in law, public administration and shorthand. Minimum entry requirements are normally five GCSEs at grades A, B or C, including English, but A-levels are usually required. All GCSE and A-level subjects are acceptable.

☛ Full-time one-year course followed by probation and a training contract on a regional or local newspaper. The qualifying period for entry for the National Certificate is 18 months. Two A-levels are required for entry to the one-year course.

☛ Degree in any subject. Graduates serve a period of probation and have a training contract. The qualifying period for entry for the National Certificate is 18 months. There are some one-year postgraduate courses in journalism. See GCSEs and higher education on page 132.

✍ **Further information** Training Department, Newspaper Society, Bloomsbury House, Bloomsbury Square, 74–77 Great Russell Street, London WC1B 3DA (please send an A4 stamped addressed envelope)

📖 **Reading** *Working In* series: *Journalism* published by and available from the Careers and Occupational Information Centre, price £2.65

☛ School careers library classification FAC

Laboratory technician work

Laboratory technicians and assistants maintain the equipment in a scientific laboratory and set up experiments. They may take readings, mix chemical solutions, prepare slides and troubleshoot experiments before they are used by classes in educational institutions. A technician may be an integral part of a research team carrying out skilled techniques within criteria laid down by professional scientists. See also Medical laboratory science work.

☛ Full-time or part-time college courses for a BTEC National Certificate/Diploma in Science. Four GCSEs at grades A, B or C, including mathematics and preferably double award science, or a BTEC First Certificate/Diploma in Science are required.

✍ **Further information** Institute of Science Technology, Mansell House, 22 Bore Street, Lichfield, Staffordshire WS13 6LP

ılıl **Reading** Fact sheets on courses in science published
by and available free from the Business and Technology
Education Council, Central House, Upper Woburn Place,
London WC1H 0HH

☛ School careers library classification QOX

Land management
see **Estate agency, auctioneering and
valuation** *and* **Surveying**

Land surveying
see **Surveying**

Landscape architecture

Landscape architects design the layout of open spaces –
these might be parks and playgrounds or the land
surrounding public buildings, power stations or factories.
They advise on the planting of trees and shrubs in such
developments.

☛ Four-year full-time or five-year sandwich course
leading to a degree in landscape architecture. Candidates
require three GCSEs at grades A, B or C and two A-levels;
most colleges require English, mathematics or science.
Other useful subjects would be art, history, biology/
botany, geography/geology and a language other than
English.

☛ A good base of GCSEs and at least two A-levels are
required for a degree in architecture, planning or a related
discipline, followed by a postgraduate course. See GCSEs
and higher education on page 132.

✍ **Further information** The Landscape Institute,
6/7 Barnard Mews, London SW11 1QU

ılıl **Reading** *Professional Careers in Landscape
Architecture, Landscape Sciences and Landscape
Management* published by the Landscape Institute. Single
copies available free

*Architecture, Landscape Architecture and Planning Degree
Course Guide* published by Hobsons Publishing PLC, price
£4.99
☞ School careers library classification UL

Language work

Translators translate written material generally into their
own language. Knowledge of another language by itself is
not sufficient; they must in addition have some specialised
knowledge – of business, science, building, engineering or law.

Simultaneous interpreters translate while a person is
speaking, usually translating into their own language.
Liaison interpreters translate into and out of two or three
languages being used in a discussion. Interpretation is a
very small field.

Bilingual secretaries work in many commercial firms
translating letters and orders and writing letters in foreign
languages. In firms that do not employ translators they
may do some translation.

Other careers where languages are useful or essential:
exporting, air cabin crew, marketing, hotel and catering
(see Catering, including hotel and institutional
management), tourism (see Travel and tourism work),
Civil Service (Diplomatic Service, Home Office), armed
forces, teaching foreign languages and international
telephone operation (GCSE French required).
☞ Full-time secretarial linguist course. Qualifications to
enter these courses range from three GCSEs at grades A, B
or C to three A-levels including two A-level languages.
☞ Full-time or part-time college courses for a BTEC
National Certificate/Diploma in Business and Finance.
Four GCSEs at grades A, B or C or a BTEC First
Certificate/Diploma are required for entry. The National
awards can be followed by a BTEC Higher National
Diploma or college diploma course in business studies
with language options, languages for business or similar

courses. These courses can also be entered with three GCSEs at grades A, B or C and one A-level.

☛ A good base of GCSEs at grades A, B or C, including English, leading to A-levels which include at least one in a foreign language. A few universities prefer one of the GCSEs to be Latin. Although it is possible to enter a degree course in foreign languages without A-level or AS in languages, this is rare. Some degree courses in modern languages concentrate on literature, while others deal with the social and economic life of the country. See GCSEs and higher education on page 132.

✍ **Further information** Institute of Linguists, 24a Highbury Grove, London N5 2EA

▥ **Reading** *Working In* series: *Languages* published by and available from the Careers and Occupational Information Centre, price £2.95

CRAC *Degree Course Guides: French; Italian and Hispanic Studies; Russian and Oriental Studies; German (including Dutch and Scandinavian Studies)* published by Hobsons Publishing PLC, price £4.99 each

☛ School careers library classification FAL

Law
see **Legal work**

Leather technology

Leather technologists apply their scientific knowledge of chemistry, physics and biology to the processes of converting hides and skins into finished leathers. These leathers are then used in other industries to produce shoes, clothes, gloves, leather goods, safety products, sports equipment and industrial leathers.

☛ Open learning courses leading to the City and Guilds Operatives' Certificate in Leather Manufacture and the City and Guilds Craft Certificate in Leather Manufacture. There are no formal entry qualifications required.

☛ Two-year block-release course for the BTEC National Certificate in Leather Technology. Four GCSEs at grades A, B or C, including chemistry, physics, mathematics and English, or a BTEC First Certificate/Diploma are required for entry.

☛ Three-year full-time course for a degree in leather technology at the British School of Leather Technology, Nene College, Northampton. Four GCSEs, including mathematics and biology, and A-level chemistry or the BTEC National Certificate are required for entry.

☛ Entry after a degree in chemistry or a suitable postgraduate course. Graduates in chemistry, chemical engineering or biochemistry may study for a degree in leather technology in one or two years or for the Associateship of the Leathersellers' Centre by research. For a degree in chemistry, a good base of GCSEs at grades A, B or C and normally A-levels in mathematics, physics and chemistry are required. See GCSEs and higher education on page 132.

✍ **Further information** The British School of Leather Technology, Nene College, Moulton Park, Northampton NN2 7AL

☛ School careers library classification SAF

Legal work

Barristers represent their clients in court. As well as advocacy they do paperwork – giving their opinion on legal matters. Clients cannot approach a barrister direct; they must do so through a solicitor.

☛ A good base of GCSEs at grades A, B or C and two or more A-levels are required for entry to a degree course (not necessarily in law). It is essential to have a first or second class honours degree in any subject. Graduates with non-law degrees must first take the one-year course for the Common Professional Examination. Everyone intending to practise at the Bar of England and Wales must then attend the one-year vocational course at the Inns of Court School of Law. Students reading for the Bar must join one of the four Inns of Court before starting the vocational stage of training and keep the required number of dining terms in their Inn of Court (ie eating a certain number of dinners at the Inn of Court they have joined). A newly qualified barrister must then spend a year as a pupil in the chambers of a practising barrister and may not do any professional work until the second six months. See GCSEs and higher education on page 132.

✍ **Further information** The Council of Legal Education, Inns of Court School of Law, 39 Eagle Street, London WC1R 4AJ

📖 **Reading** *The Bar into the '90s* published by and available free from the General Council of the Bar, 3 Bedford Row, London WC1R 4AJ

☛ School careers library classification LAB

Legal executives work in solicitors' offices and legal departments and usually specialise in a particular area of work – divorce, litigation (taking cases to court), conveyancing (buying and selling houses) or wills and probate (dealing with matters when someone dies). They interview clients and submit papers to court. They do not represent clients in court.

☛ Part-time, day-release or evening classes at a college of further education for the Institute's examinations. Four academic GCSEs at grades A, B or C, including English, are required. Practical subjects such as art, drama, food and nutrition, technology, textiles and woodwork may not be acceptable as it depends on the syllabus covered; further details from the Institute. For students without four GCSEs there are one-year part-time courses for the Preliminary Certificate in Legal Studies. To qualify as a legal executive applicants must be working in a legal department or a solicitor's office.

✍ **Further information** Institute of Legal Executives, Kempston Manor, Kempston, Bedford MK42 7AB

📖 **Reading** *Opening the Way to a Career in Law* and *From School to a Career in Law* published by and available free from the Institute

☛ School careers library classification LAD

Solicitors carry out a wide range of legal work, and normally act on the instructions of clients. Clients can ask for any legal service, from buying a home to selling a company. A solicitor's role is to give legal advice and representation, and matters can vary from crime to conveyancing, from making a will to carrying out a multi-million pound deal. At present solicitors represent their clients in the lower courts, hiring a barrister for representation in the higher courts, but in due course solicitors will have the right of representation in the higher courts.

☛ A good base of GCSEs at grades A, B or C and at least two A-levels are required for a degree in any subject. This should be followed by a one-year course for the Common Professional Examination (or equivalent), a further year for the new Legal Practice Course and then two years in a Training Contract with a firm of solicitors or other approved organisation. See GCSEs and higher education on page 132.

☛ A good base of GCSEs at grades A, B or C and normally three A-levels at high grades (subjects rarely specified) for a law degree. The degree should be followed by the new one-year Legal Practice Course and then two years in a Training Contract with a firm of solicitors or other approved organisation. See GCSEs and higher education on page 132.

☛ It is possible to qualify as a solicitor after working as a fully qualified legal executive. Candidates who are over 25 and have worked for five years in a solicitor's office and have Fellowship status of the Institute of Legal Executives can either take the Legal Practice course or can enter two-year training and take the Legal Practice course externally.

✍️ **Further information** The Law Society, 113 Chancery Lane, London WC2A 1PL

The Law Society's Careers and Recruitment Service, 227/228 Strand, London WC2R 1BA

📖 **Reading** *Solicitors – A Career for Tomorrow* published by and available free from the Law Society's Careers and Recruitment Service

☛ School careers library classification LAC

Library and information management

Professional entry

Librarians and information professionals are responsible for selecting, buying, organising and using all kinds of materials and media which record information. They work in public libraries, schools, universities, colleges, industry and commerce, the media, national libraries and museums – in fact for any organisation that has information needs. The use of computers is integral to modern practice. See also Information science.

☛ Three- or four-year Library Association accredited university or college of higher education degree course in information studies. A good base of GCSEs at grades A, B or C and at least two A-levels or a BTEC National award are normally required for entry.

☛ A degree in any subject followed by a one-year Library Association accredited postgraduate course in information studies. See GCSEs and higher education on page 132. Graduates may then work towards gaining the professional qualifications offered by the Library Association through the award of Chartered Membership and entry to its Professional Register.

Para-professional entry

Library and information assistants support library and information managers by carrying out the more routine work. Many assistants are not qualified but can study for vocational qualifications whilst in post.

☛ Full-time or part-time college courses for a BTEC National Certificate/Diploma in Business and Finance with options in library and information work. Four GCSEs at grades A, B or C, including English and mathematics, are required for entry. Alternatively the City and Guilds Library Assistants' Certificate or a BTEC First Certificate/Diploma will be accepted for entry. With a BTEC National award with appropriate options it will be possible to be considered for degree courses in librarianship on a par with A-level holders.

✍ **Further information** The Library Association, 7 Ridgmount Street, London WC1E 7AE

▥ **Reading** Various career leaflets published by and available from the Library Association

☛ School careers library classification FAF

Local government administration

People working in local government administration are employed by local authorities who run a wide range of public services including museums, libraries, education, refuse collection and street cleaning, parks, social services, swimming pools and sports centres. Increasingly local authority services are being put out to tender so that private firms can compete for the work. Many professional posts in local authorities are dealt with under the appropriate career: these include accountancy, social work, planning, housing management and environmental health.

Administrative grade

☛ Full-time or part-time college courses for a BTEC National Certificate/Diploma in Public Administration or Business and Finance. Four GCSEs at grades A, B or C, including English and mathematics, or a BTEC First Certificate/Diploma are required for entry. This can be followed by a part-time course for the BTEC Higher National Certificate in public administration options. These courses can also be entered with three GCSEs at grades A, B or C and one A-level.

☛ Two-year full-time or three-year sandwich course for the BTEC Higher National Diploma in Public Administration. Three GCSEs at grades A, B or C and one A-level or a BTEC National Award are required for entry.

☛ Degree in any subject for entry to administrative trainee schemes run by local authorities. Some authorities may prefer trainees who have taken degrees such as public administration. See GCSEs and higher education on page 132.

Clerical grade

☛ One-year part-time course for the BTEC First Certificate or one-year full-time or two-year part-time course for the BTEC First Diploma in Business and Finance. There are no formal entry requirements but many colleges require two or three GCSEs at grade E or above, including English. Many local authorities lay down entry requirements of GCSEs at grades A, B or C for the clerical grade.

✍ **Further information** The Local Government Management Board, Arndale House, Arndale Centre, Luton, Bedfordshire LU1 2TS

▥ **Reading** Leaflets published by and available free from the Local Government Management Board

Working In series: *Local Government* published by and available from the Careers and Occupational Information Centre, price £2.95

☛ School careers library classification CAG

Marine engineering
see **Engineering**

Marines
see **Royal Navy and Royal Marines**

Market research

Market researchers find out what consumers want and why. They want to know the demand that exists for their products and services; how their products compare with competitors'; how different types of advertising and packaging affect sales. There are many ways of collecting this information: the best known is by interviewing the public. Trained interviewers are employed on a part-time basis. Research executives guide the project through its various stages, designing the questionnaire and analysing and reporting the findings.

☞ A good base of GCSEs at grades A, B or C, including mathematics, and two or more A-levels are required. Most executive-level posts require a degree in any subject. There are openings for market research assistants with GCSEs and A-levels. See GCSEs and higher education on page 132.

✍ **Further information** Market Research Society, 15 Northburgh Street, London EC1V 0AH

📖 **Reading** *A Career in Market Research* and *What is Market Research?* published by and available free from the Society

☞ School careers library classification OB

Marketing

Marketing managers find out what potential customers wish to buy, develop products or services to cater for this and plan and co-ordinate the work of the various departments of a company to make the product or service available at the right price.

☞ Two-year part-time course for the Qualifying Certificate of the Institute of Marketing. Students must be at least 18 and have one A-level and four GCSEs at grades A, B or C, including English and a numeracy subject; other suitable subjects would be single or double award science, history, geography, economics, business studies and foreign languages. All subjects are acceptable. This can be followed by a further year's study for entry to the Diploma of the Institute. Alternative qualifications for entry to the Diploma course include BTEC Higher awards in Business and Finance with a marketing orientation or a degree.

☛ Part-time or full-time college courses for the BTEC National Certificate/Diploma in Business and Finance. Four GCSEs at grades A, B or C, preferably including English and mathematics, or a BTEC First Certificate/ Diploma are required for entry. This can be followed by BTEC Higher awards with marketing options and/or professional qualifications.

☛ A degree in any subject followed by a graduate traineeship or a degree in business studies with marketing options followed by a traineeship. Marketing degrees are now being offered by some higher education institutions. A good base of GCSEs at grades A, B or C and at least two A-levels are required to enter a degree course. See GCSEs and higher education on page 132.

✍ **Further information** The Chartered Institute of Marketing, Moor Hall, Cookham, Berkshire SL6 9QH

▥ **Reading** *Working In* series: *Marketing* published by and available from the Careers and Occupational Information Centre, price £2.95

☛ School careers library classification OB

Materials science and metallurgy

Materials scientists apply the science of physics and chemistry to all materials – metal and non-metals. They work both in the production of the material and its processing into finished products. Metallurgists are concerned with the extraction of metals from their ores, and the composition and uses of metals and alloys. Other materials scientists apply similar principles to other materials, particularly polymers, ceramics and glass.

In 1992 the Plastics and Rubber Institute and the Ceramics Institute merged with the Institute of Metals to form the Institute of Materials.

Materials science technician

☞ Full-time or part-time college course for a BTEC National Certificate/Diploma in Metals Technology or Materials Technology. Four GCSEs at grades A, B or C, including mathematics and at least single award science, or a BTEC First Certificate/Diploma are required for entry. The BTEC National Certificate can be followed by a two-year part-time course for the Higher National Certificate or a four-year part-time or three-year sandwich course for the Higher National Diploma.

Materials technologist/metallurgist

☞ Two-year full-time, three-year sandwich course or four-year part-time course for the BTEC Higher National Diploma in Metals Technology or Materials Technology. Candidates require either a BTEC National Certificate/ Diploma with appropriate units or A-level study of chemistry and physics with a pass in one of these subjects and a GCSE at grade A, B or C in mathematics. Holders of the BTEC Higher National Diploma qualify for the Associateship of the Institute.

☞ Degree in metallurgy or materials science. A good base of GCSEs at grades A, B or C is required. A-levels in physics, chemistry and mathematics are generally required. See GCSEs and higher education on page 132 about entry to higher education. With an accredited classified honours degree in metallurgy or materials science the holder can become a Corporate Member of the Institute.

✍ **Further information** The Institute of Materials, PO Box 471, 1 Carlton House Terrace, London SW1Y 5DB
☛ School careers library classification QOS

Mathematics

Mathematicians are employed to solve problems in engineering, computing, medicine, economics, marketing, physics and statistics and to analyse mathematical data. Most routine work is done by computers.

☛ Two-year full-time or three-year sandwich course for the BTEC Higher National Diploma in Mathematics, Statistics and Computing. An A-level pass in mathematics with at least 50% pure mathematics content and an adequate command of English are required or a BTEC National Certificate/Diploma with appropriate modules.

☛ A good base of GCSEs at grades A, B or C and at least two A-levels, preferably including more than one mathematics A-level, are required for a degree in mathematics. See GCSEs and higher education on page 132.

✍ **Further information** Institute of Mathematics and its Applications, 16 Nelson Street, Southend-on-Sea, Essex SS1 1EF
Mathematical Association, 259 London Road, Leicester LE2 3BE

▥ **Reading** *Qualifications and Careers in Mathematics* published by and available from the Institute of Mathematics and its Applications, price £8.00
Careers for the Mathematically Qualified published by and available free from the Mathematical Association
Working In series: *Mathematics* published by and available from the Careers and Occupational Information Centre, price £2.50
☛ School careers library classification QOG

Mechanical engineering
see **Engineering**

Medical laboratory science work

Medical laboratory scientific officers work in hospital pathology and other medical laboratories. They analyse blood, study tissues removed in operations, study bacteria and viruses and undertake chemical analyses of urine and body fluids. To become a professionally qualified Medical Laboratory Scientific Officer a degree is required. There are posts in hospital laboratories for those with lower-level qualifications.

☞ A good base of GCSEs at grades A, B or C leading to specialisation in A-level science subjects is required to enter an accredited degree course in biomedical sciences. These courses provide exemption from the first year of the three-year Fellowship programme of the Institute. A list of these courses is available from the Institute. Degree courses where the principal subject is animal physiology, biochemistry, biology, chemistry, microbiology, physics or zoology can be followed by study for the Fellowship of the Institute. All the degree courses must be approved by the Medical Laboratory Technicians Board at the Council for Professions Supplementary to Medicine. See GCSEs and higher education on page 132.

✍ **Further information** Institute of Medical Laboratory Sciences, 12 Queen Anne Street, London W1M 0AU

▥ **Reading** *Medical Laboratory Scientific Officers and Clinical Laboratory Support Services (HSC 22)* published by the Department of Health and available free from Health Service Careers, PO Box 204, London SE5 7ES Leaflets published by and available free from the Institute
☞ School careers library classification JAX

Medical records work

Medical records officers compile and maintain medical records in hospitals and health centres.

☛ Part-time, day-release or correspondence course for the Diploma examinations of the Association. To take the Diploma five GCSEs at grades A, B or C are required, including English and mathematics.The following subjects are not acceptable: child development, drama, electronics, engineering, music and photography.

✍ **Further information** Association of Health Care Information and Medical Records Officers, Pear Tree Cottage, Mill Lane, Horsemans Green, Whitchurch, Shropshire SY13 3EA

▥ **Reading** *A Worthwhile Career in Health Care Information and Medical Records* published by and available free from the Association; a stamped addressed envelope is required if requesting information

☛ School careers library classification CAV

Medicine and surgery

Doctors diagnose and treat physical and mental disorders. They can work as general practitioners (GPs) running surgeries and visiting patients in their own homes or can work in hospitals where they specialise in a medical field such as paediatrics (child health), geriatrics (medical care of old people), psychiatry (mental health) or surgery (operations). A few doctors work in community health where the emphasis is on preventing disease.

☛ A good base of GCSEs at grades A, B or C, including English, mathematics and double award science, followed by A-levels which should include chemistry. Fewer than half the medical schools now insist on three A-level science subjects including chemistry. It would be wise to plan to study physics and biology beyond the level of double award science – by taking these subjects at AS level, for example. A five-year degree course is essential to qualify as a doctor; practical hospital experience is also required. See GCSEs and higher education on page 132.

✍ **Further information** British Medical Association, Tavistock Square, London WC1H 9JP

Information sheets available on request from the British Medical Association (please send a large stamped addressed envelope)

📖 **Reading** *Learning Medicine* published by and available from the British Medical Association, price £4.95

Medicine Degree Course Guide published by Hobsons Publishing PLC, price £4.99

☛ School careers library classification JAB

Merchant Navy

Deck officers navigate the ship and are responsible for loading and unloading the cargo.

Engineer officers operate and maintain the ship's engines.

Electro-technical/radio officers operate and maintain the ship's radio and radar; vacancies are limited.

Ratings are able seamen who work under the direction of the officers. Shipping companies, while recruiting British officers, often recruit ratings from overseas.

Catering ratings prepare food for members of the crew.

Deck officers

All deck officer cadets must be in good health and have good eyesight.

☛ Three-and-a-half-year sandwich course with periods of on-the-job training on board ship and periods of study in approved nautical colleges leading to the BTEC National Diploma in Nautical Science together with the Department of Transport Class 4 Certificate of Competency and ultimately a Higher National Diploma. Four GCSEs at grades A, B or C, including mathematics, double award science, English or a subject testing command of English, are required. Entry is as a deck officer with a shipping company.

☛ A scheme similar to the BTEC Diploma course leads directly to the Department of Transport Class 3 Certificate of Competency. For this, candidates require three GCSEs at grades A, B or C and must have studied two A-levels and obtained a pass in one. One A-level must be mathematics or a physical science.

☛ Three-year full-time or four- to six-year sandwich course leading to a degree in nautical studies. Three GCSEs at grades A, B or C and two A-levels are the minimum requirement. Some colleges require mathematics and physics at A-level. All require some evidence of study of both these subjects beyond GCSE, eg AS.

☛ Other schemes exist for which the minimum entry requirement is three GCSEs at grade E or above in mathematics, science and a subject testing command of English.

Engineer officers

☛ A sandwich course with periods of on-the-job training on board ship and periods of study in approved colleges and engineering workshops is taken. Successful completion of this course enables students to study for the BTEC Higher National Certificate or Diploma in Marine Engineering. The BTEC awards provide certain exemptions from the Department of Transport Engineers Class 2 Certificate and in certain cases from parts of the Engineers Class 1 Certificate. A minimum of four GCSEs at grades A, B or C, including mathematics and science, is required for entry to the Higher National Certificate course. For entry to the Higher National Diploma course one A-level in either mathematics or physics is also required, the other A-level subject having been studied to this level but not necessarily passed. Entry is as an engineer officer cadet with a shipping company. The holder of the Department of Transport Engineers Second Class Certificate can register as a Technician Engineer with the Engineering Council, the holder of a First Class

Certificate can register as an Incorporated Engineer and the holder of the Extra First Class Certificate can register as a Chartered Engineer. See Engineering.

Dual certificate officer (deck and engineer)

☞ Four- to five-year sandwich course with periods at sea and periods at nautical college. Four GCSEs at grades A, B or C in mathematics, double award science and a subject testing command of English, and mathematics and physics studied to A-level and a pass in one are required.

Electro-technical officer/radio officer

☞ Three-year full-time course at an approved college. After the second year, successful students gain the BTEC National Diploma in Marine Radio and Radar; after the third year the BTEC Higher National Certificate in Marine Radio and Radar. Three GCSEs at grades A, B or C in mathematics, science and English are generally required for entry. Candidates cannot go to sea until they have successfully completed the course.

Junior deck, engine room and catering ratings

☞ Shipping company sponsorship is essential before enrolment at the National Sea Training College, Gravesend. This formerly single sex college now has an intake of 10% women and trains future seamen/women and stewards, the latter with progression to ship's cook. There are no academic entry requirements but shipping companies normally expect candidates to have GCSEs at grade D or above in mathematics, science and a subject testing command of English. Applicants must be in good health (and have good eyesight for the deck department). There are no longer any age limits.

✍ **Further information** Individual shipping companies, whose addresses can be obtained from the *Annual Directory of Shipowners, Shipbuilders and Marine Engineers* (The Blue Book) which should be available in large public libraries. The names and addresses of the companies participating in the training scheme can be obtained from the Co-ordinating Agent, Government Assistance for Training, 30/32 St Mary Axe, London EC3A 8ET

☛ School careers library classification YAL

Metallurgy
see **Materials science and metallurgy**

Meteorology

Meteorologists provide weather information and carry out research into the atmosphere. The main employer is the Meteorological Office which is a government department.

☛ For entry as an Assistant Scientific Officer a minimum of four GCSEs at grades A, B or C, including English and physics/double award science or mathematics (preferably both), are required. Study concessions leading to higher qualifications such as the BTEC Higher National Certificate may be granted to suitable staff.

☛ For entry as a Scientific Officer a degree (BTEC Higher National Diploma or Certificate may possibly be acceptable) in mathematics, physics, meteorology, computer science or electronics is required. In general, these courses require a good base of GCSEs at grades A, B or C and at least two A-levels in mathematics and physics. See GCSEs and higher education on page 132. For both Assistant Scientific Officer and Scientific Officer posts most successful applicants have qualifications above the minimum.

✍ **Further information** Meteorological Office Recruitment, London Road, Bracknell, Berkshire RG12 2SZ

☛ School careers library classification QOL

Midwifery

A midwife works with expectant mothers in the ante-
natal clinic that mothers attend before the baby is born.
The midwife delivers the baby – unless there are
complications, when a doctor is called. Generally babies
are delivered in hospital but there are a few home births.
The midwife then looks after the mother and the newly
born baby for not less than 10 days, and sometimes up to
the limit of 28 days.

☛ Three-year full-time course for those without
previous nursing experience. Five GCSEs at grades A, B or
C, including English and at least single award science, are
required. The demand for places is such that
qualifications above the minimum are often necessary.
Minimum age is $17^1/_2$.

☛ Eighteen months' full-time course for registered
general nurses (see Nursing). The majority of midwives
qualify in this way.

☛ Four-year degree course combining nursing and
midwifery qualifications. Three GCSEs at grades A, B or
C in English, mathematics and at least single award
science and two A-levels are required.

✍ **Further information** English National Board for
Nursing, Midwifery and Health Visiting, Careers
Advisory Centre, PO Box 356, Sheffield S8 0SJ

▥ **Reading** *Registered Midwife (HSC 3)* published by the
Department of Health and available free from Health
Service Careers, PO Box 204, London SE5 7ES

☛ School careers library classification JAD

Mine engineering
see **Engineering**

Mine surveying
see **Surveying**

Museum work

People working in museums and art galleries organise, acquire, catalogue and display the exhibits. They may put on special exhibitions, run museum clubs for children or liaise with schools. Some curators are allowed time to do their own research work. Conservation officers repair and restore exhibits.

☛ On-the-job training as museum assistant. Recruitment to the large national museums was formerly carried out by the Civil Service and there were standard entry requirements. National museums now recruit their own personnel and there are no nationally laid down requirements. Normally museums would be expecting four GCSEs at grades A, B or C as a minimum; in practice most successful candidates have degrees.

☛ Two-year full-time college course for a BTEC Higher National Diploma in Conservation Studies. A foundation course in art and design, a BTEC National award or exceptionally one A-level is required for entry. Three-year full-time degree course in conservation, candidates straight from school require a minimum of two A-levels and a range of GCSEs at grades A, B or C. These courses lead to posts as conservation officers in museums for which there are few vacancies.

☛ A degree in any subject (competition for posts is keen and subjects such as history of art, social history, arts administration, archaeology, zoology and geology may be preferred). This can be followed either by a one-year university postgraduate course in museum studies or by direct entry.

☛ The Museums Association Diploma is being phased out. The Museum Training Institute has been set up to offer flexible training. Successful completion will lead to the MTI Certificate of Competence which will be validated by the National Council for Vocational Qualifications.

✍ **Further information** Museums Association,
42 Clerkenwell Close, London EC1R 0PA
Museum Training Institute, 55 Well Street, Bradford
BD1 5PS

📖 **Reading** *Careers in Museums* published by and
available free from the Museums Association or Museum
Training Institute (please send a large stamped addressed
envelope)

☛ School careers library classification FAE

Music

Professional musicians work as composers, performers –
playing instruments, singing and conducting – and
teachers. Performers may work in large orchestras or in
small groups. This is a highly competitive career.

☛ Two- to four-year full-time course at a music college.
Entrance is by competitive audition, although in practice
most successful candidates will also have a good base of
GCSEs at grades A, B or C and one or more A-levels. If the
student wishes to combine musical performance and
teaching in a state school, GCSEs at grades A, B or C in
English and mathematics are required.

☛ Three-year full-time course for a degree in music, a
degree where music is combined with other subjects or a
performing arts degree. A good base of GCSEs at grades
A, B or C and at least two A-levels are required. A-level
music is usually required for a degree in music.

✍ **Further information** Incorporated Society of
Musicians (ISM), 10 Stratford Place, London W1N 9AE
(careers only)

📖 **Reading** *Careers with Music* published by and
available free from the Incorporated Society of Musicians
(ISM)

Working In series: *Music* published by and available from the
Careers and Occupational Information Centre, price £2.65

☛ School careers library classification GAD

Nature conservation

Assistant regional officers in English Nature work to preserve plant and animal life; they survey and assess the priorities in their area, liaise with local planning authorities and give advice to schools. **Wardens** undertake practical conservation work in nature reserves and liaise with neighbouring landowners. These are very popular careers and there is strong competition for the few vacancies. There are also posts, often seasonal, working for nature organisations.

Assistant regional officers
☛ A good base of GCSEs at grades A, B or C and A-levels in the biological sciences, environmental science or geography are required for entry to a degree in the biological sciences, horticulture, ecology or environmental sciences. See GCSEs and higher education on page 132.

Wardens
☛ On-the-job training. Minimum age is 26. Candidates should be keen naturalists interested in field studies, able to drive and maintain vehicles and have experience of estate work. In practice most successful candidates have at least A-level standard in biology and many are graduates.
✍ **Further information** English Nature, Northminster House, Peterborough PE1 1UA
▥ **Reading** *Working In* series: *Environment* published by and available from the Careers and Occupational Information Centre, price £2.95
☛ School careers library classification WAR

Naval architecture
see **Engineering**

Navy

see **Royal Navy and Royal Marines**

Neurophysiology technology work

A more familiar name for the neurophysiology technologist is the EEG (electro-encephalography) technologist, who is responsible for setting up and operating electronic equipment which records the electrical activity of the brain and nervous system.

☛ Two-year part-time day-release or block-release course for the BTEC National Certificate in Science (physiological measurement options) while working for a hospital or a regional health authority. Four GCSEs at grades A, B or C are required, including English, mathematics and double award science. The National Certificate may be followed by the BTEC Higher National Certificate in Physiological Measurement.

✍ **Further information** Electro-Physiological Technologists' Association (EPTA), Neurophysiology Department, Selly Oak Hospital, Birmingham B29 6JD

▥ **Reading** *A Career in Clinical Neurophysiology* published by and available free from EPTA

Medical Technical Officers and Assistants (HSC 13) published by the Department of Health and available free from Health Service Careers, PO Box 204, London SE5 7ES

☛ School careers library classification JOB

Nursery nursing

Nursery nurses work with children under eight; they do not generally nurse sick children, although some find employment in hospitals as play therapists. They work in nursery schools and classes with children between the ages of three and five, and in day nurseries, which take children under five all day. They also work as nannies in private households and in crèches attached to leisure centres and further education colleges and in many other settings.

☛ Two-year full-time college course (as it is in a modular format it can be taken part-time in up to five years) with practical experience in an approved setting for the Diploma or Preliminary Diploma in Nursery Nursing. (From September 1994 this will be in conjunction with NVQ Level 3 in Child Care and Education.) Students progress from the Preliminary Diploma to the Diploma by completion of an intensive extra term or part-time study over a year. There are no nationally set entry requirements but some colleges require two or more GCSEs at grades A, B or C. Minimum age is 16.

☛ Twenty-four-month or longer full-time diploma course at a private nursery training college affiliated to the Association of Nursery Training Colleges. Three GCSEs at grades A, B or C, including English, are required. Minimum age is 18.

✍ **Further information** National Nursery Examination Board, 8 Chequer Street, St Albans, Hertfordshire AL1 3XZ

▥ **Reading** *Nursery Nursing* – a *Life with Children* published by and available free from the National Nursery Examination Board (please send a large stamped addressed envelope)

☛ School careers library classification KEB

Nursing

Nurses help to care for patients with mental and physical disorders both in the community and in hospital.

☛ Three-year full-time registered general nurse training in a hospital. A minimum of five GCSEs at grades A, B or C is required. No particular subjects are specified; however, most schools of nursing now require applicants to have five academic GCSEs at grades A, B or C, including English and mathematics and/or single or double award science. Very popular nurse training schools may require A-levels. Minimum age is 17¹/₂.

☛ A good base of GCSEs at grades A, B or C and at least two A-levels are required for a four-year degree course in nursing. A-levels in physics, chemistry and biology are preferred; if these A-levels are not held, science GCSEs are required. See GCSEs and higher education on page 132.

☛ Three-year full-time course in a college of nursing which is linked to a college of higher education or a university. Students will receive a non-means-tested bursary and gain clinical experience in hospitals and in the community. These new courses are known as Project 2000 and will run alongside the traditional training and will eventually replace it. Entry qualifications are five GCSEs at grades A, B or C.

✍ **Further information** Regional health authorities, addresses in telephone directories
English National Board for Nursing, Midwifery and Health Visiting, Careers Advisory Service, PO Box 356, Sheffield S8 0SJ

▥ **Reading** *Registered General Nurse/Registered Mental Nurse/Registered Nurse for the Mentally Handicapped (HSC 2)* published by the Department of Health and available free from Health Service Careers, PO Box 204, London SE5 7ES

☛ School careers library classification JAD

✆ccupational therapy

The occupational therapist's aim is to enable those who are temporarily or permanently disabled to be as independent as possible in their everyday lives, whilst recovering from illness or adapting to disability.

☛ Three-year full-time course at a recognised school attached to a hospital or university. Five GCSEs at grades A, B or C, including English and at least one science subject, and two academic A-levels are required.

✍ **Further information** College of Occupational Therapists, 6–8 Marshalsea Road, Southwark, London SE1 1HL

📖 **Reading** *The Occupational Therapist* available free from the College of Occupational Therapists (please send a stamped addressed envelope)

☛ School careers library classification JAR

Operational research

Operational researchers often use mathematical and computer-based models in helping decision-makers in industry, commerce, government and public service to solve complex problems, many of which entail a significant degree of risk or uncertainty.

☛ A degree with some mathematical or statistical study is essential; some degree courses include options in operational research. A good base of GCSEs at grades A, B or C, including mathematics, and A-levels in mathematics, science, social science or economics are required. See GCSEs and higher education on page 132.

✍ **Further information** Operational Research Society, Neville House, Waterloo Street, Birmingham B2 5TX

📖 **Reading** *A Career in Operational Research* published by and available free from the Operational Research Society

☛ School careers library classification COF

Optometry (ophthalmic optics)

Optometrists (ophthalmic opticians) test and examine eyes and prescribe spectacles and contact lenses.

☛ Three-year full-time degree course in optometry (ophthalmic optics) for which three GCSEs at grades A, B or C and generally three A-levels are required, two of which must be chemistry, mathematics, physics or biology. Subjects not held at A-level should be held at GCSE if possible.

✍ **Further information** The British College of Optometrists, 10 Knaresborough Place, London SW5 0TG

▥ **Reading** *A Career in Vision Care* published by and available free from the General Optical Council, 41 Harley Street, London W1N 2DJ

☛ School careers library classification JAL

Ordnance Survey work
see **Cartography**

Organisation and methods and work study

Work study officers study how work is done and suggest methods to improve efficiency. Organisation and methods officers apply the same techniques to office work.

☛ Full- or part-time course for Part I of the Diploma in Administrative Management of the Institute of Administrative Management. Four GCSEs at grades A, B or C, including English, and one A-level or an appropriate BTEC National is required for entry.

☛ Part-time, full-time or sandwich course for the BTEC National Certificate/Diploma in Business and Finance. Four GCSEs at grades A, B or C, including English and mathematics, are required. This may be followed by study for BTEC Higher National Certificates/Diplomas which may include options in work study or organisation and methods. The courses leading to the Higher awards may also be entered by candidates with one A-level.

☛ One-year part-time study, distance learning or a short concentrated course for the Management Services Certificate of Competence. Ideally candidates should have several GCSEs, including English and mathematics, and

one or more A-levels or a BTEC National in Business and
Finance. Entry to management services is usually based
on maturity and experience in handling people, and
typically new entrants will have a degree or a BTEC
Higher award. The Certificate can be followed by two-
year part-time study for the Diploma in Project
Management.

☛ A degree in any subject or an appropriate professional
qualification, eg in banking or accountancy, followed by
either on-the-job training or part-time study for the
examinations of the professional institutes.

✍ **Further information** Institute of Administrative
Management, 40 Chatsworth Parade, Petts Wood,
Orpington, Kent BR5 1RW

Institute of Management Services, 1 Cecil Court, London
Road, Enfield, Middlesex EN2 6DD

▥ **Reading** *Choosing a Career in Management Services*
published by and available free from the Institute of
Management Services

☛ School careers library classification COD

Orthoptics

Orthoptists work as part of the eye-care team, diagnosing
and treating defects of binocular vision, eg squints and
disorders of eye muscle movements. A lot of the work is
with children, in both hospitals and health centres, but
more adult patients are being referred for assessment and
treatment.

☛ Full-time three-year orthoptics degree course at
Liverpool and Sheffield Universities and Queen's College,
Glasgow. Five GCSEs at grades A, B or C, including
English, mathematics and preferably double award
science, and three A-levels, preferably including biology,
are normally required.

✍ **Further information** British Orthoptic Society,
Tavistock House North, Tavistock Square, London WC1 9HX

⚏ **Reading** *Orthoptist (HSC 16)* published by the Department of Health and available free from Health Service Careers, PO Box 204, London SE5 7ES
☞ School careers library classification JAL

Osteopathy

Osteopaths treat people using their hands and pay particular attention to the effects that muscles and ligaments have on joint movement. Osteopaths do not work within the National Health Service.
☞ Four-year full-time course for which five GCSEs at grades A, B or C, including English, and two A-levels, preferably in chemistry and biology, are required. All GCSE subjects are acceptable. This course leads to the degree in osteopathy recognised by the General Council and Register of Osteopaths.
✍ **Further information** The British School of Osteopathy, 1–4 Suffolk Street, London SW1Y 4HG
⚏ **Reading** Leaflet published by and available free from the British School of Osteopathy
☞ School careers library classification JOD

Painting and decorating
see **Building crafts**

Patents

Patent agents advise their clients on patent law: for example, whether a 'new' invention has already been patented and therefore is not really new. They do similar work with trademarks and industrial design. Their main work is drafting the description of the invention which forms the basis of the protection given by the patent. They operate in private practice or in large industrial firms. **Patent examiners** work in the Patent Office and examine applications for patents to ensure that only really 'new' inventions qualify for granted patents.

Patent agents

☛ A degree course in science, applied science, mathematics or engineering is virtually essential. A good base of GCSEs at grades A, B or C for A-level specialisation in sciences and/or mathematics will be required for entry to a degree course. See GCSEs and higher education on page 132. The degree should be followed by three years' study for the Institute's examinations while working in a suitable office. After passing the Institute's examinations a patent agent will be able to work in this country, but to practise before the European Patent Office a further examination must be passed. It is possible to sit the Institute's examinations without a degree but nowadays very few people do so.

Patent examiner

☛ A first or second class honours degree in science, engineering, mathematics or an equivalent professional qualification is required. On-the-job training is given. See GCSEs and higher education on page 132.

✍ **Further information** The Chartered Institute of Patent Agents, Staple Inn Buildings, High Holborn, London WC1V 7PZ

The Principal Examiner (Administration), The Patent Office, Concept House, Cardiff Road, Newport, Gwent NP9 1RH (for patent examiners)

📖 **Reading** *Patent Agency – a Career for You?* published by and available free from the Chartered Institute of Patent Agents

Patent Examiner – A Career as a Patent Examiner published by and available free from the Patent Office

☛ School careers library classification LAK

Personnel work

Personnel managers recruit and select staff, run staff
training programmes and negotiate with trades unions
about pay and working conditions. They work in local
authorities and hospitals, as well as in commercial and
industrial concerns.

☞ Part-time or full-time study for the examinations of
the Institute of Personnel Management. To become a
student member you will normally need to have three
GCSEs at grades A, B or C and two A-levels (no subject to
be counted at both levels), or to have passed the
Certificate in Personnel Practice course. No academic
qualifications are required to enter the one-year
Certificate in Personnel Practice course.

☞ Part-time or full-time course for the BTEC Higher
National Certificate/Diploma in Business and Finance; it
is possible to take modules specialising in personnel work.
Three GCSEs at grades A, B or C and one A-level or a
BTEC National award are required for entry. This should
be followed by study for the Institute's examinations.
BTEC Higher award holders may be given exemptions.

☞ Degree in any subject followed either by a
postgraduate course in personnel management and/or
full-time or part-time study for the Institute's
examinations. Accreditations towards the Institute's
examinations may be granted to holders of certain
postgraduate diplomas.

☞ Degree in human resource management, public
administration or business studies followed by part-time
or full-time study for the Institute's examinations.
Accreditation may be granted towards the Institute's
examinations for candidates with appropriate degrees. See
GCSEs and higher education on page 132.

✍ **Further information** Institute of Personnel
Management, IPM House, Camp Road, Wimbledon,
London SW19 4UX

▊▊▊ Reading Leaflets published by and available free from
the Institute
☞ School careers library classification CAS

Pharmacy

Pharmacists prepare medicines from natural and
synthetic products and dispense them to the public. Most
pharmacists work in community pharmacies (retail
chemists' shops) and are involved not only in dispensing
medicines and counselling patients on their proper use,
but also in advising the public on a variety of health care
issues. Hospital pharmacists, in addition to dispensing
medicines, advise their medical and nursing colleagues on
the effects of medicines and warn them of any toxic side-
effects. Industrial pharmacists are involved in a wide
variety of occupations: research, production, marketing,
general administration and technical and medical
information.

☞ A pharmacy degree and one year's pre-registration
training (ie paid practical training) are essential for
registration as a pharmaceutical chemist. A good base of
GCSEs at grades A, B or C and three A-levels, one of
which must usually be chemistry, the others chosen from
physics, a mathematical subject and a biological subject,
are required. See GCSEs and higher education on page
132.

✐ **Further information** Royal Pharmaceutical Society of
Great Britain, 1 Lambeth High Street, London SE1 7JN

▊▊▊ Reading *Pharmacy and Pharmacology Degree Course
Guide* published for CRAC by Hobsons Publishing PLC,
price £4.99

Pharmacy: Effective Caring and *Entrance Requirements to
Schools of Pharmacy* published by and available free from
the Royal Pharmaceutical Society of Great Britain

☞ School careers library classification JAG

Pharmacy technician work
see **Dispensing assistant/pharmacy technician work**

Photography

Photographs are required for advertising, illustration, portraits (especially at weddings) and scientific and medical work. Photographers may process the photographs themselves or employ technicians to do this.

☛ Three-year part-time or one- to two-year full-time courses for the City and Guilds Certificate No. 747 Professional Photography. Entry qualifications vary but can be as high as three GCSEs at grades A, B or C.

☛ Full-time or part-time college courses for a BTEC National Certificate/Diploma in Design (Photography) or Photographic Technology. Four GCSEs at grades A, B or C or a BTEC First Certificate/Diploma are required for entry.

☛ Two-year full-time course for the BTEC Higher National Diploma in Photography. A BTEC National Certificate/Diploma with appropriate units or a foundation course in art and design is required for entry. Generally candidates straight from school should have three GCSEs at grades A, B or C and two A-levels. Some colleges specify certain GCSE subjects such as art, English, mathematics and science. Some colleges will accept candidates with one A-level. In some colleges the two-year course can be followed by an additional year's course leading to the Professional Qualifying Examination of the British Institute of Professional Photography.

☛ Three-year full-time course for a degree in photography. A good base of GCSEs at grades A, B or C and two A-levels, a BTEC National Diploma, satisfactory completion of a foundation course in art and design together with five GCSEs at grades A, B or C or three GCSEs at grades A, B or C and one A-level.

For all the photography courses above, most colleges also expect candidates to have a portfolio of work to show at the interview.

☛ Three-year full-time course for a degree in photographic sciences. Three GCSEs at grades A, B or C, including chemistry, mathematics and physics, and two A-levels including at least one of these subjects. A-levels in all three are preferred.

Press photography

☛ One-year full-time course for press photographers. One A-level and four GCSEs at grades A, B or C, including English, are required. An 18-month qualifying period on a regional or local newspaper is required before sitting the National Certificate examination.

☛ Direct entry with five GCSEs at grades A, B or C, including English, two years' photographic experience or after taking a further education course in photography. Training is by block release. A two-year qualifying period is required before sitting the National Certificate examination.

✍ **Further information** British Institute of Professional Photography, Fox Talbot House, 2 Amwell End, Ware, Hertfordshire SG12 9HN

Royal Photographic Society, The Octagon, Milsom Street, Bath BA1 1DN

For press photographers: Training Department, The Newspaper Society, Bloomsbury House, Bloomsbury Square, 74–77 Great Russell Street, London WC1B 3DA (please send a large stamped addressed envelope)

▥ **Reading** *Getting Jobs in Photography*, price £4.50 and *An Eye for the Job*, price 75 pence, both published by and available from the British Institute of Professional Photography

☛ School careers library classification EV

Physics

Physics is the study of matter and energy. Physicists apply their knowledge in fields as diverse as electronics, optics, acoustics and medical physics.

☞ If you are planning from the outset to be a professional physicist you should take a degree course in physics or applied physics at a university or college of higher education. A good base of GCSEs at grades A, B or C and specialisation in mathematics and physics at A-level will be required. See GCSEs and higher education on page 132.

☞ Two-year full-time or equivalent part-time course for the BTEC National Certificate/Diploma in Science. Four GCSEs at grades A, B or C, including mathematics and a science subject, or a BTEC First Certificate/Diploma are required for entry. The BTEC National awards can be followed by study for the BTEC Higher National Certificate or Higher National Diploma in Science (Physics) for which three GCSEs, including mathematics and a subject testing command of English, A-level physics and mathematics studied beyond GCSE are alternative entry qualifications.

✍ **Further information** The Institute of Physics, 47 Belgrave Square, London SW1X 8QX

▥ **Reading** *Physics and Physicists, What is Physics?, What do Physicists Do?, Working in Physics* and *A Day in the Life* published by and available free from the Education Department, The Institute of Physics

☞ School careers library classification QOF

Physiological measurement
see **Cardiology technician work** *and* **Neurophysiology technology work**

Physiotherapy

Physiotherapists work under the direction of a doctor,

treating injuries and disease with exercises, massage and electrotherapy.

☛ Three- or four-year full-time approved degree course at a training school attached to a hospital or university. A minimum of five GCSEs at grades A, B or C and two A-levels, preferably including biology, are required. The GCSEs must include English and double award science.

✍ **Further information** Chartered Society of Physiotherapy, 14 Bedford Row, London WC1R 4ED

▥ **Reading** Leaflets published by and available from the Society

☛ School careers library classification JAN

Piloting
see **Air piloting**

Planning
see **Town planning**

Plastering
see **Building crafts**

Plastics and rubber technology and engineering
see **Materials science and metallurgy**

Police and security services

The police maintain law and order by preventing and detecting crime. They work in traffic control, in the CID or with young people. Security officers work for private security firms guarding premises and transporting large amounts of cash from banks and other businesses.

Police

☛ Two-year on-the-job training includes courses at a training centre after passing an entrance examination. Four GCSEs at grades A, B or C, including English and mathematics, may give exemption from the entrance examination but most forces require all candidates to sit the entrance examination. All GCSE subjects are acceptable. Minimum age is 18$\frac{1}{2}$. Candidates must be physically fit and meet the minimum height and eyesight standards.

☛ Cadet force entry is normally between 16 and 18$\frac{1}{2}$ years. Training combines educational studies, physical and adventure training together with community service and instruction in police work. Many forces prefer candidates with some GCSEs, not necessarily at grades A, B or C.

☛ A degree in any subject plus selection tests for the Special Course leading to accelerated promotion. See GCSEs and higher education on page 132.

The Metropolitan Police of London recruit cadets nationwide but all other police forces recruit cadets from their force area only.

Security officers

☛ Each firm lays down its own entrance requirements but preference is given to candidates with some GCSEs at grade E and above.

✍ **Further information** Police Recruiting Department, Home Office, 50 Queen Anne's Gate, London SW1H 9AT

▥ **Reading** Working In series: *Police and Security* published by and available from the Careers and Occupational Information Centre, price £2.50

☛ School careers library classification MAB

Polymer technology
see **Materials science and metallurgy**

Post Office work

Post Office counters

Counter clerks work behind Post Office counters carrying out many types of business transactions – selling stamps and postal orders; accepting parcels; paying pensions and allowances; dealing with National Girobank and National Savings Bank accounts; issuing licences and British visitors' passports.

Royal Mail

Letters administrators carry out office duties.
Postmen and **postwomen** collect, sort and deliver the mail.
☞ For counter clerks the Post Office recruits people of a good educational standard, eg four GCSEs including English and mathematics. However, formal qualifications are not essential as all applicants must pass an aptitude test which measures the skills needed for the job. Those successful in the test will be invited to interview.
☞ For postmen and postwomen preference is normally given to candidates with some GCSEs at grade E and above.
✍ **Further information** Local Divisional Personnel Units
▥ **Reading** Leaflets published by the Post Office and available free from your local Divisional Personnel Unit
☞ School careers library classification CAM/YAT

Poultry farming
see **Farming and agricultural advisory work**

Printing

Printing firms produce a wide range of printed material from the obvious books, newspapers and magazines to labels, wallpaper, cardboard boxes and plastic bags. Computers are an integral part of the modern printing process.

The work is prepared by craft-level workers in the printing preparation trades of planners, plate-makers, compositors, camera operators and scanner operators. Printing machine operatives in lithography, letterpress or photogravure who are skilled craft-level operatives run the printing presses. The work then passes to the Finishing Department, books are bound by hand or machine and the finishing machine operators fold, stitch and trim. Printing technologists or managers supervise the whole process. After discussion with the customer, they choose the most suitable paper and printing medium for the job, estimate the final cost and ensure a smooth workflow.

Printing crafts

☞ Since 1983 the old apprenticeship system in printing has been replaced by a system where the length of training depends on the time needed to reach standards of competence. Recruits to most printing crafts are now called trainees; those in the print preparation trades are 'agreement trainees'. All trainees under 18 have to complete a college-based course, the first term of which is usually full-time, followed by periods of block-release study in the other five terms. Generally the courses lead to City and Guilds Certificates and a National Vocational Qualification. Most employers prefer candidates with GCSEs at grade D or above in English, mathematics, technology and double award science. For the print preparation trades good spelling and the ability to handle delicate materials, such as film and photographic paper, are essential. Machine operatives should also have good colour vision. In London and the South East there are regional selection tests including colour vision and intelligence tests followed by interviews. The British Printing Industries Federation then compiles a register of suitable candidates from which employers select trainees.

✍ **Further information** British Printing Industries Federation, 11 Bedford Row, London WC1R 4DX

▥ **Reading** A careers pack is published by and available free from the British Printing Industries Federation

☞ School careers library classification SAR

Printing technology

☞ Full-time and part-time college courses for the BTEC National Diploma/Certificate in Printing. Four GCSEs at grades A, B or C, a BTEC First Certificate/Diploma or a City and Guilds Certificate are required for entry. The BTEC National awards can be followed by a BTEC Higher National Diploma/Certificate. These courses can also be entered with three GCSEs at grades A, B or C, including mathematics and science, and one appropriate A-level.

☞ Four-year sandwich course for a degree in printing technology. A good base of GCSEs at grades A, B or C, including mathematics, and at least two A-levels, including one from chemistry, mathematics or physics, are required. See GCSEs and higher education on page 132.

✍ **Further information** Institute of Printing, 8 Lonsdale Gardens, Tunbridge Wells, Kent TN1 1NU

☞ School careers library classification SAR

Typography

☞ Courses leading to BTEC National Diploma/ Certificates, Higher National Diplomas or degrees in art and design specialising in graphic design. See Art and design for details of entrance requirements.

✍ **Further information** Chartered Society of Designers, 29 Bedford Square, London WC1B 3GG

Society of Typographic Designers, New Inn Lane, Avening, Tetbury, Gloucestershire GL8 8NB

☞ School careers library classification ED, or under printing SAR

Prison work

Prison officers are in charge of the day-to-day care of the prisoners. Governors and assistant governors are in overall charge of the prison, remand centre, youth custody or detention centre.

☛ For prison officers: on-the-job training generally lasting three months. The first month is spent at a nearby prison or youth custody centre and the next two months at a prison officers' training school. There are no specific entry requirements but reasonable proficiency in reading, writing, spelling and arithmetic is needed to pass the aptitude test. Minimum age is 21.

☛ Prison officers can be promoted to assistant governor. For direct entry as an assistant governor there are no specific educational requirements but in practice most successful candidates for the accelerated promotion scheme have degrees or equivalent qualifications.

✍ **Further information** The Recruiting Office, The Home Office (Prison Service), Cleland House, Page Street, London SW1P 4LN

▥ **Reading** *The Inside Story* (prison officers) and *Inside Management* (assistant governors) published by and available free from the Home Office

☛ School careers library classification MAD

Probation and after-care work
see **Social work**

Producing
see **Drama, Film and video production** *and* **Broadcasting: radio and television**

Psychology

Psychologists should not be confused with psychiatrists,

who are doctors who treat the mentally ill. Psychologists study human behaviour and apply their knowledge in the fields of educational, clinical or occupational psychology. Educational psychologists work for local education authorities advising on children's emotional and behavioural problems and running the School Psychological Service. Clinical psychologists are employed in the NHS helping people with behavioural and emotional problems. Occupational psychologists are trained to help people adapt to their work environment. They also try to adjust the environment to the needs of those who work in it.

☞ A degree in psychology and postgraduate training is essential. A good base of GCSEs, including mathematics, and at least two A-levels are required. Some courses require science A-levels so it would be wise to have double award science among your GCSE subjects. See GCSEs and higher education on page 132.

✍ **Further information** The British Psychological Society, St Andrew's House, 48 Princess Road East, Leicester LE1 7DR

▥ **Reading** *How about Psychology?* published by and available from the British Psychological Society, price £1.95 *Psychology Degree Course Guide* published by Hobsons Publishing PLC, price £4.99

☞ School careers library classification KEL

Public health inspection
see **Environmental health**

Public relations

A public relations officer's job, whether employed in house or as a consultant, is to promote the organisation he or she serves. This is done by preparing publications, organising exhibitions, answering queries from the public and liaising with the media.

☛ Full-time or part-time college courses for a BTEC National Certificate/Diploma in Business and Finance. Four GCSEs at grades A, B or C, preferably including English and mathematics, or a BTEC First Certificate/Diploma are required for entry. This can be followed by either a course for a BTEC Higher National Certificate/Diploma or by study for the CAM Certificate (see below).

☛ Two years' day-release or evening study for the Communication, Advertising and Marketing Education Foundation (CAM) Certificate in Communication Studies. The subjects studied are: marketing; advertising; public relations; media; research and behavioural studies; sales promotion and direct marketing. All students must be 18 years old or above. They must have three GCSEs at grades A, B or C and two A-levels or five GCSEs and have been employed in a relevant field for one year of a BTEC National Certificate/Diploma in Business and Finance. All students must hold English GCSE at grades A, B or C. The CAM Diploma in Public Relations involves a further year's study. In addition, students must have four years' experience.

☛ A degree in any subject. See GCSEs and higher education on page 132. Some degrees in business studies give exemptions from the CAM examinations. There are some degree courses which specialise in public relations. Most entrants to PR work are graduates. Fluency in speech and writing is essential. There is keen competition for vacancies. For membership of the Institute, four years' experience is also required.

✍ **Further information** Institute of Public Relations, The Old Trading House, 15 Northburgh Street, London EC1V 0PR

▥ **Reading** *Public Relations as a Career* published by and available free from the Institute

☛ School careers library classification OG

Publishing

Publishers select or commission manuscripts from authors and arrange for their printing. They organise the distribution and marketing of finished books.

☛ Virtually no editorial posts in publishing firms are open to school-leavers; experience as a publisher's representative or bookshop assistant can be a useful introduction to the marketing department of a publishing firm.

☛ Degree in any subject plus some specialised knowledge for editorial work. There are very few posts in editorial departments and competition is extremely fierce. See GCSEs and higher education on page 132. Some people enter editorial work after secretarial work in publishers' offices.

✍ **Further information** The Publishers' Association, 19 Bedford Square, London WC1B 3HJ

▥ **Reading** *Careers in Book Publishing* published by and available free from the Publishers' Association (please send a stamped addressed envelope)

Working In series: *Publishing* published by and available from the Careers and Occupational Information Centre, price £2.95

☛ School careers library classification FAD

Purchasing and stock control

Purchasing officers work for large organisations. Their task is to buy raw materials for manufacturing, goods which are to be resold and articles for use in the organisation, ranging from large items of equipment to office stationery. As supplies are often bought in bulk, special terms are negotiated. They may also be responsible for stock control, the management of stores and the distribution of goods.

☛ Four or five years' part-time study for the Institute's examinations while working in a suitable post. Three GCSEs at grades A, B or C, including English and mathematics or another quantitative subject, and two A-levels are required. All subjects are acceptable. Very few entrants qualify this way; the majority take further or higher education.

☛ Full-time or part-time college course for a BTEC National Certificate/Diploma in Business and Finance. Four GCSEs at grades A, B or C, preferably including English and mathematics, or a BTEC First Certificate/ Diploma are required. The BTEC National awards can be followed by BTEC Higher awards which may contain options in purchasing. Courses leading to BTEC Higher awards may also be entered with three GCSEs at grades A, B or C and one A-level. BTEC Higher awards should be followed by study for the Institute's examinations; some BTEC options will give some exemptions from the Institute's examinations.

☛ A degree in any subject followed by one or two years' part-time study for the Institute's examinations. Some exemptions can be granted from the Institute's examinations for candidates with a degree in business studies with suitable purchasing options. For some posts a degree in engineering or applied science is valuable. See GCSEs and higher education on page 132.

✍ **Further information** Institute of Purchasing and Supply, Easton House, Easton on the Hill, Stamford, Lincolnshire PE9 3NZ

▥ **Reading** *Purchasing and Supply: A Career Worth Thinking About* published by and available free from the Institute

☛ School careers library classification OP

Quantity surveying
see **Surveying**

Quarrying

Quarrying is extracting stone, slate, marble, gravel and
sand from the surface by drilling, blasting, cutting, etc.
These materials are used for constructing buildings and
roads. People working in quarrying sometimes have
qualifications in engineering (see Engineering).

☛ Three-year sandwich course at Doncaster
Metropolitan Institute of Higher Education for the BTEC
Higher National Diploma for which three GCSEs at
grades A, B or C and one A-level are required. The A-level
must be either mathematics or physics, the other subject
having been studied to that level. The course can also be
entered by students holding a BTEC National
Certificate/Diploma in mining or engineering.

✍ **Further information** The Institute of Quarrying,
7 Regent Street, Nottingham NG1 5BY

☛ School careers library classification ROB

Radio
see **Broadcasting: radio and television**

Radio engineering
see **Broadcasting: radio and television,
Engineering** *and* **Merchant Navy**

Radiography and radiotherapy

Diagnostic radiographers and therapy radiographers
work under the direction of a doctor. The diagnostic
radiographer takes X-rays to help the doctor diagnose
illness and injuries. The therapy radiographer treats
patients using radiation.

☛ Three-year full-time course in either diagnostic
radiography or therapeutic radiography at a recognised

school or centre in a hospital or university. Candidates have to comply with normal university admission requirements: two A-levels and three GCSEs at grades A, B or C or three A-levels and one GCSE at grade A, B or C. Additionally candidates who have gained eight points with one A-level, ie at grade A or B, satisfy the minimum requirement of the College of Radiographers. Schools of Radiography set their own course requirements which are in practice higher. Your GCSEs should include English, mathematics and double award science.

✍ **Further information** College of Radiographers, 14 Upper Wimpole Street, London W1M 8BN

▥ **Reading** *Radiography* published by the Department of Health and available free from Health Service Careers, PO Box 204, London SE5 7ES

☞ School careers library classification JAP

Recreation management

Recreation managers (also known as leisure or amenity managers) work for local authorities, commercial companies and voluntary bodies managing sports, recreation and leisure centres, swimming pools, urban and country parks, sports grounds and entertainment, cultural, arts and community centres.

☞ Part-time study for the examinations of the Institute of Leisure and Amenity Management (ILAM). There are four ILAM qualifications: to study for the First Award four GCSEs at grades A, B or C or a BTEC First award are required. All GCSE subjects are acceptable. Pre-entry requirements for the Certificate in Leisure Operations are two A-levels or a BTEC National award in Leisure Studies. Pre-entry requirements for the Certificate in Leisure Management include Higher National awards in appropriate subjects and leisure related degree courses. Finally to enter the Diploma in Leisure Management either an ILAM Certificate must be held or certain degree and postgraduate qualifications. For each level certain other qualifications are acceptable – details from ILAM.

☞ Management training scheme for the Institute of Baths and Recreation Management which consists of four modules studied part-time at college or by correspondence. The minimum recommended entry level is four GCSEs, including English and mathematics, and one A-level or BTEC National Diploma/Certificate.

☞ A degree in any subject or a comparable qualification followed by a one-year postgraduate course. There are also degree courses in leisure and recreation studies and in arts administration. See GCSEs and higher education on page 132.

✍ **Further information** Institute of Leisure and Amenity Management (ILAM), Lower Basildon, Reading, Berkshire RG8 9NE

Institute of Baths and Recreation Management, Giffard House, 36/38 Sherrard Street, Melton Mowbray, Leicestershire LE13 1XJ

▥ **Reading** *Careers in the Leisure Industry* published by and available from ILAM

☞ School careers library classification GAJ

Religious work

Christian church work

Ordained ministers preach the faith, conduct services, baptisms, weddings and funerals as well as provide a social service, visiting the ill and the bereaved. In addition to the ordained ministry there are other openings for full-time work in the church for both men and women. These include youth work, social work, missionary work and parish work for which a wide range of professional qualifications is required, although there are, in some cases, denominational training courses. In the Roman Catholic church only men may at present be ordained as priests. In other churches women and men may be

ordained as priests, ministers, deacons or accredited lay
workers.

☛ Those entering the ministry take a course at a
theological or bible college. The length of the course and
the qualifications required depend on the candidate's age
and denomination. Many candidates have already taken a
university degree course (see GCSEs and higher education
on page 132), but candidates without higher education
qualifications should still apply.

✍ **Further information** The Vocations Officer, Advisory
Board of Ministry, Church House, Great Smith Street,
London SW1P 3NZ (Church of England)

Secretary for Ministry, The Baptist Union, Baptist House,
129 Broadway, PO Box 44, Didcot, Oxfordshire OX11 8RT

The Methodist Church, Division of Ministries, Room 509,
25 Marylebone Road, London NW1 5JR

The United Reformed Church, Ministerial Training
Committee, 86 Tavistock Place, London WC1H 9RT

Diocesan Vocations Service, 31 Moor Road, Headingley,
Leeds LS6 4BG (RC)

For other religious faiths please consult your local place
of worship

☛ School careers library classification FAM

Residential care
see **Social work**

Retail and wholesale distribution

Over two million people work in distribution – in small
shops, large department stores, in mail-order firms and in
wholesalers. Most have contact with the customers but
buyers, who purchase stocks, do not meet the public.
There are jobs in retailing for people at all levels of
educational attainment. Some sales assistants know little
about the products they sell, but many have specialised

knowledge acquired on the job and on special training courses. There are many careers in retailing that are not dealt with in this section – display work, which includes window dressing, is under Art and design; also look at the sections on Personnel work, Purchasing and stock control and Accountancy.

☛ One-year full-time or two-year part-time college courses for a BTEC First Certificate/Diploma in Distribution Studies. There are no formal entry requirements but colleges may prefer students with some GCSEs at grade E or above. Many 16 and 17 year-old school-leavers are entering retailing through Youth Training (YT). The BTEC First Certificate/Diploma may be part of the training scheme.

☛ Full-time and part-time college courses for a BTEC National Diploma/Certificate in Distribution Studies. Four GCSEs at grades A, B or C or a BTEC First Certificate are required for entry.

☛ Two-year part-time course for BTEC Higher National Certificate, two-year full-time, three-year sandwich or three-year part-time course for BTEC Higher National Diploma. Entry requirements are three GCSEs at grades A, B or C and one A-level or an appropriate BTEC National Certificate or Diploma.

☛ A degree in any subject followed by on-the-job training and specialised courses. See GCSEs and higher education on page 132. A degree in business studies (in some colleges you can take optional subjects in distribution) would be particularly relevant. One university has a degree course in licensed retailing and other colleges and universities have specialised degree courses.

There are many training schemes run by specialised bodies, eg for selling wines and spirits, jewellery or flowers.

✍ **Further information** Distributive Industries Training Trust, 5 Bridge Street, Bishop's Stortford, Hertfordshire CM23 2JU

📖 **Reading** *Working In* series: *The Retail Industry*

published by and available from the Careers and
Occupational Information Centre, price £2.50
There's a Great Career in Store for You published by and
available free from the Distributive Industries Training
Trust
☛ School careers library classification OE

Royal Air Force

National defence is the main task of all branches of HM
Forces. There are many different professional posts in the
Royal Air Force apart from flying; these include
administration, catering and medicine.

Officers

☛ Five GCSEs at grades A, B or C, including English and
mathematics, and two A-levels at grade E or better are
required; the subjects must not overlap significantly in
content and only one may be non-academic. The age
limits for the General Duties (Flying) Branch are $17^1/_2$–24
for pilots and 26 for navigators. The age limits for the
Administrative Branch, General Duties (Ground) Branch
(which includes air traffic control and fighter control
duties) are $17^1/_2$–30.
☛ The RAF can sponsor students for sixth-form study
and on degree courses. See GCSEs and higher education
on page 132.

Airmen/women

☛ Entry requirements for aircrew who fly as crew on
planes are three GCSEs at grades A, B or C, including
mathematics and English. Age limits are $17^1/_2$–26. At least
an elementary knowledge of science is required.
☛ For ground trades there are various entry
requirements. Age limits are usually $16^1/_2$–39. Candidates
for technician training require up to four GCSEs at grades
A, B or C, including mathematics and a physics-based
science subject.

Women have equal pay and can be employed on the same duties as men, with the exception of RAF Regiment, Fire and Aerial Erector. This may change in the next few years so that all careers in the RAF are open to women.

✍ **Further information** Local RAF Careers Information Office (look under 'Royal Air Force' in the telephone directory)

▥ **Reading** A range of booklets is published by the Ministry of Defence and is available free from the RAF Careers Information Offices

☛ School careers library classification BAL

Royal Navy and Royal Marines

The Royal Navy is concerned with defence while the Merchant Navy transports cargo and passengers around the world (see Merchant Navy).

Naval officers
Full career commissions: Seaman, Engineering (mechanical and electrical), Supply and Secretariat and Royal Marines

☛ The Scholarship scheme for A-level study is limited to seamen, aircrew and engineering entrants. Five GCSEs at grades A, B or C are required. The age limits are 15–17.

☛ Naval College entry: five GCSEs at grades A, B or C and two A-levels are required for all entries. For Seamen and Supply and Secretariat, English and mathematics must be included. For Engineering the A-levels must be mathematics and physics and GCSE English is also required. The age limits are 17–23.

☛ University/college of higher education cadetship entry: candidates must obtain a place on a degree course or be already taking a degree course. They are awarded for all branches except instructor.

☞ Graduate entry: candidates must also have GCSEs at grades A, B or C in English and mathematics. The age limit is 26. Higher age limits for instructors, medical officers and dental officers. See GCSEs and higher education on page 132.

Short career commissions
Naval College entry:

☞ **Seaman:** five GCSEs at grades A, B or C required, including English and mathematics. Age limits 17–26.

☞ **Engineering:** three GCSEs at grades A, B or C, including English, and two A-levels in mathematics and physics are required. A BTEC National Certificate/Diploma in subjects appropriate to further mechanical or electrical specialisation is an alternative entry qualification. Age limits 17–26.

☞ **Royal Marines:** A minimum of five GCSEs at grades A, B or C, including English and mathematics, are required. Age limits 17–23, 25 for graduates.

Instructor, medical and dental officers and chaplains

☞ A good base of GCSEs at grades A, B or C, A-levels and higher education are essential. See Teaching, Medicine and surgery, Dentistry and Religious work.

Ratings and marines

☞ The majority of ratings must pass a selection test but do not need GCSE qualifications. There are a few exceptions to this general rule.

Women join the Navy on exactly the same terms as men. The Women's Royal Naval Service (WRNS) no longer exists as a separate service.

✍ **Further information** The Director, Naval Recruiting, Old Admiralty Building, London SW1A 2BE

▥ **Reading** A range of booklets is published by the Ministry of Defence and is available free from your local Royal Navy Careers Office

☛ School careers library classification BAB

Rubber technology

see **Materials science and metallurgy**

afety work

Safety officers are employed by industrial and commercial organisations to check that safe systems of work are used, that accidents are reported and that the legal requirements are met.

Factory inspectors are civil servants who visit industrial premises to ensure that the provisions of the Health and Safety at Work Act are being complied with.

☛ Part-time courses for the examinations of the National Examination Board in Occupational Safety and Health which leads to membership of the Institution of Occupational Safety and Health.

☛ Two-year on-the-job training for candidates for the factory inspectorate who have a good base of GCSEs at grades A, B or C, including mathematics, and a degree, BTEC Higher National Diploma, an equivalent or higher qualification in science or technology and three years' practical experience in industry.

☛ Full-time course for a degree in occupational safety and health. Contact the Institution for full details.

✑ **Further information** Health and Safety Executive, Personnel Management, St Hugh's House, Bootle, Merseyside L20 3QY

Institution of Occupational Safety and Health, 222 Uppingham Road, Leicester LE5 0QG

▥ **Reading** *Health and Safety at Work: Advice, Investigation and Enforcement* published by and available free from the Health and Safety Executive

☛ School careers library classification COT

Science
see **Biochemistry, Biology, Chemistry, Laboratory technician work** *and* **Physics**

Sculpture
see **Art and design**

Secretarial work

Secretarial work covers a wide range of employment that can be entered at almost every level of educational attainment. **Copy typists** type texts from handwritten or previously typed drafts; they may also do some filing. **Audio typists** type material from pre-recorded tapes. **Shorthand typists** take dictation in shorthand and type out the text later. The amount of responsibility that a secretary is given varies. Some do shorthand typing, filing and make appointments, whereas others may be able to work more on their own initiative. They may answer some letters themselves, prepare agendas and keep minutes of meetings. **Bilingual secretaries** may do some translation work. Being able to operate a word processor is now essential. A word processor is basically a keyboard – which looks very much like a typewriter – attached to a screen and a printer. The text is displayed on the screen so mistakes can be easily corrected. The machine has a 'memory' so text can be stored to be used many times, perhaps with slight changes each time. You should try to learn a word processing language such as WordPerfect.

☛ Direct entry with GCSE subjects and some typing skills. This will usually lead to posts as copy, audio or shorthand typists and not to secretarial posts.

☛ Part-time or full-time course in shorthand and typing at a college of further education. GCSEs at grade E or above may be required. This will usually lead to posts as copy, audio or shorthand typists and not to secretarial posts.

☞ Full-time courses at colleges of further education that lead to posts as secretaries generally demand at least four GCSEs at grades A, B or C. Secretarial courses including foreign languages require GCSE or A-level language study.

☞ Two-year part-time course for the BTEC National Certificate or two-year full-time or three-year sandwich course for the BTEC National Diploma in Business and Finance taking secretarial options. It is possible to specialise in agricultural secretarial work. The majority of the work as a farm secretary involves accounts and figure work to a greater degree than most other secretarial jobs. The BTEC courses give students wider knowledge of the business world and can also be used as an entry qualification for higher level courses. Four GCSEs at grades A, B or C, preferably including English and mathematics, or a BTEC First award are required for entry.

☞ Two-year part-time course for the BTEC Higher National Certificate or two-year full-time, three-year sandwich or three-year part-time course for the BTEC Higher National Diploma in Business and Finance. It is possible to specialise in personal/private secretarial work. Three GCSEs at grades A, B or C, one A-level or a BTEC National award are required for entry.

☞ A degree in any subject followed by a secretarial course designed for graduates. Some are specifically for graduates in foreign languages. See GCSEs and higher education on page 132.

☞ Two-year full-time course for the Diploma of the Association of Medical Secretaries. Four GCSEs at grades A, B or C, including English, are required. Special provision is made for A-level entry candidates who are expected to complete the course in one year.

☞ One-year full-time course for the National Certificate for Farm Secretaries. Three GCSEs at grades A, B or C, including English and mathematics (or a subject demonstrating numeracy), are required. Minimum age is 17.

☛ Many school-leavers are entering office work under the Youth Training (YT) Office Studies Scheme.

✍ **Further information** Association of Medical Secretaries, Practice Administrators and Receptionists, Tavistock House North, Tavistock Square, London WC1H 9LN

Institute of Agricultural Secretaries, NAC, Stoneleigh, Kenilworth, Warwickshire CV8 1LZ

▥ **Reading** *Working In* series: *Offices* published by and available from the Careers and Occupational Information Centre, price £2.50

☛ School careers library classification CAT

Shipbroking

Shipbrokers act as intermediaries between shipowners and people who have cargo to be sent abroad by sea. They are paid commission by the shipowner. They also represent the shipowner while the ship is in port and may arrange matters such as customs formalities or the loading of cargo. They may also buy and sell ships on behalf of owners or manage ships for their owners.

☛ Part-time study at a college of further education or by a correspondence course for the Membership Examinations of the Institute of Chartered Shipbrokers. Normally two A-levels or their equivalent are required.

✍ **Further information** The Institute of Chartered Shipbrokers, 3 Gracechurch Street, London EC3V 0AT

▥ **Reading** Leaflet published by and available free from the Institute

☛ School careers library classification YAS

Social work

Social workers help people to adjust to their social and personal problems. They are employed by local authority social services departments, education authorities, the probation service and many voluntary bodies. They work in area offices and often visit families in their homes. They also work in residential homes, day centres, hospitals, child guidance clinics and prisons. They train to work with people of all ages and of all types.

Qualifying training

☞ The Diploma in Social Work (DipSW) is a new social work qualification. It replaces the Certificate in Social Services (CSS) and the Certificate of Qualification in Social Work (CQSW). DipSW training can be college-based or employment-based. The DipSW can be taken as part of a DipHE, a degree or a postgraduate qualification. Applicants under 21 for DipSW programmes require a good base of GCSEs and two A-levels or the equivalent. Mature students do not require formal qualifications but must demonstrate their ability to study at an advanced level. All applicants are usually required to have had some voluntary or paid work experience in social services or a related field.

Non-qualifying training

☞ Courses leading to CCETSW's Preliminary Certificate in Social Care (PCSC) are run for 16–19 year-olds in colleges of further education. The PCSC is not a qualification but the course offers students the chance to learn about social services work while continuing their general education. There are no formal entry requirements but colleges often ask for some GCSEs at grade E or above.

☞ Full-time or part-time college course for BTEC First Certificate/Diploma in Caring. There are no formal entry requirements but many colleges ask for some GCSEs at grade E or above. This can be followed by the BTEC National Certificate/Diploma in Caring Services (Social Care). An alternative entry requirement for the BTEC National course is four GCSEs at grades A, B or C. A BTEC National award will often be accepted as an entry qualification for a DipSW programme.

✍ **Further information** Central Council for Education and Training in Social Work (CCETSW), Information Service, Derbyshire House, St Chad's Street, London WC1H 8AD

CCETSW Information Service, Block B, 2nd Floor, South Gate House, Wood Street, Cardiff CF1 1EW

⩕ **Reading** *Working In* series: *Social Work* published by and available from the Careers and Occupational Information Centre, price £2.50

☛ School careers library classification KEB

Speech and language therapy

A speech and language therapist is professionally qualified to identify, assess and treat communication disorders in children and adults. The speech and language therapist has to work closely with members of the medical, teaching, psychological and other caring professions. While most speech therapists work in hospitals and community clinics they may also be found in schools, special units and adult training centres.

☛ Three- or four-year full-time degree course. A good base of GCSEs at grades A, B or C, including English, a foreign language, mathematics and double award science, and at least two A-levels are normally required. Some institutions require biology at A-level. See GCSEs and higher education on page 132.

✍ **Further information** College of Speech and Language Therapists, 7 Bath Place, Rivington Street, London EC2A 3DR

☛ School careers library classification JAS

Stage management
see **Drama**

Statistics

Statisticians collect and interpret numerical data.

☛ A professional statistician needs a degree in statistics or in mathematics with statistics options. Entry requirements for a three- or four-year full-time or sandwich degree are a good base of GCSEs at grades A, B or C and at least two A-levels including mathematics. Alternatively, a first degree in mathematics, economics or some science disciplines can be followed by a postgraduate course in statistics. See GCSEs and higher education on page 132.

☛ Part-time courses for the examinations of the Institute of Statisticians. The minimum entry requirement is two GCSEs at grades A, B or C in mathematics and English; in practice most candidates have much higher entry qualifications. The final part of the Institute's examination is equivalent to an honours degree in statistics.

☛ Full-time or part-time study for the BTEC Higher National Certificate/Diploma in Mathematics, Statistics and Computing. Three GCSEs at grades A, B or C and A-level mathematics or a BTEC National award with a sufficiently high mathematical content are required for entry. The Higher award courses can be followed by study for examinations of the Institute of Statisticians.

✍ **Further information** The Institute of Statisticians, 43 St Peter's Square, Preston, Lancashire PR1 7BX

▥ **Reading** *Careers in Statistics* published by and available from the Institute of Statisticians, price £1.75
Statistics and Your Career published by and available free from the Royal Statistical Society, 25 Enford Street, London W1H 2BH

☛ School careers library classification QOG

Stock Exchange work

The London Stock Exchange is the central market place

for securities: stocks and shares in public limited companies and government securities known as 'gilts'. Careers are either within the London Stock Exchange itself or in one of its member firms which are all over the UK and the Republic of Ireland.

☛ The traditional roles of jobber and broker have been replaced by the broker/dealer. All broker/dealers must now take examinations before being allowed to trade or offer investment advice. There are no formal entry qualifications but confidence in working with numbers and good communication skills are vital. In practice many entrants have received higher education.

✍ **Further information** Public Information, The London Stock Exchange, Old Broad Street, London EC2N 1HP

📖 **Reading** *Working In* series: *Money Business* published by and available from the Careers and Occupational Information Centre, price £2.50

☛ School careers library classification NAL

Surveying

Building surveying

Building surveyors inspect buildings and make reports on their structural condition. They can advise clients on the suitability of a building for specific purposes, prepare schemes for conversion or repair and advise on costs. This job is often combined with estate agency or valuation – see Estate agency, auctioneering and valuation.

☛ Part-time study for the examinations of the Association of Building Engineers. Three GCSEs at grades A, B or C and two A-levels are required. Mathematics, an appropriate science subject and a subject requiring the use of descriptive English must be included at either level. A BTEC National Certificate/Diploma in Construction or Surveying may be an alternative entry qualification.

☛ Part-time study for the examinations of the Architects' and Surveyors' Institute. The educational requirements are under review – details from the Institute.

☞ Three-year full-time or four-year sandwich degree course in building surveying. Three GCSEs at grades A, B or C and two A-levels are required. English or English literature and mathematics must be passed at either level. These degree courses give various exemptions from the examinations of the professional bodies; details from the individual professional bodies. See GCSEs and higher education on page 132.

Agricultural land surveying and land agency

An agricultural surveyor inspects and values agricultural land, farm buildings and stock. Land agents manage farms and estates.

☞ Three- or four-year degree or diploma course in land economy or land management. A good base of GCSEs including mathematics and English and at least two A-levels are required; in some colleges preference is given to candidates with mathematics A-level. These courses give various exemptions from the examinations of the professional bodies; details from the individual professional bodies. See GCSEs and higher education on page 132.

Land surveying

Land surveyors measure the land and all the physical features so that maps can be prepared. There is little demand for land surveyors in this country and most posts are overseas. See also Cartography.

☞ Part-time study for the examinations of the Association of Building Engineers (see above under Building surveying).

☞ Three-year full-time degree course in surveying and mapping sciences or land surveying. A good base of GCSEs at grades A, B or C, including English or English literature, mathematics and physics, is required together with two A-levels in mathematics and either physics or geography. A BTEC Certificate/Diploma with a significant content of mathematics and physics is an alternative entry qualification. Approved degree courses will exempt candidates from the examinations of the Royal Institution of Chartered Surveyors.

Quantity surveying

Quantity surveyors work out the costing of a building project and are employed either in private practice or in firms of architects or civil engineers. Construction surveyors are quantity surveyors working for building firms. They are responsible for financial management, especially for the preparation of tenders that are submitted to clients to obtain work.

☛ Three-year full-time or four-year sandwich course for a degree in quantity surveying giving exemption from RICS examinations. A good base of GCSEs at grades A, B or C and at least two A-levels are required. See GCSEs and higher education on page 132.

☛ Part-time study for the examinations of the Construction Surveyors' Institute. Four GCSEs at grades A, B or C, including mathematics, English and a science, are preferred. Students should be in approved employment and/or following an approved full-time or part-time course.

✍ **Further information** The Royal Institution of Chartered Surveyors, Surveyor Court, Westwood Way, Coventry CV4 8JE

Association of Building Engineers, Jubilee House, Billing Brook Road, Weston Favell, Northampton NN3 3NW

The Construction Surveyors' Institute, Wellington House, 203 Lordship Lane, London SE22 8HA

Architects' and Surveyors' Institute, 15 St Mary Street, Chippenham, Wiltshire SN15 3JN

▥ **Reading** *Making Land, Property and Construction Work* published by and available free from the Royal Institution of Chartered Surveyors

☛ School careers library classification UM

Surveying technician work

A surveying technician works under the direction of a chartered surveyor.

☛ Full-time or part-time course for the BTEC National Certificate/Diploma in Building Studies, Land Administration, Agriculture or Surveying. Four GCSEs at grades A, B or C, including mathematics, a subject testing command of English and for building preferably double award science, are required. An alternative entry requirement is BTEC First Certificate/Diploma in Construction for which there are no formal entry requirements, although some colleges may prefer applicants with some GCSEs at grade E or above. The BTEC National awards can be followed by a BTEC Higher National Certificate/Diploma and by the Joint Royal Institution of Chartered Surveyors/Society of Surveying Technicians' Test of Competence.

✍ **Further information** Society of Surveying Technicians, Drayton House, 30 Gordon Street, London WC1H 0BH

☛ School careers library classification UM

Teaching

Teachers work in a variety of schools and colleges ranging from small nursery schools to large sixth-form colleges. Primary teachers cover most subjects while secondary teachers specialise.

☛ Four-year full-time Bachelor of Education (BEd) degree course at a college of higher education or university. Three A-levels and one GCSE at grades A, B or C or two A-levels and three GCSEs at grades A, B or C are the normal minimum entry requirements. These passes must include English, science and mathematics at either level. Students may opt to train to teach lower or upper primary school children or a limited range of subjects in secondary schools.

☛ A degree relevant to the school curriculum and a one-year college-based postgraduate education course. All students must normally have GCSEs at grades A, B or C in English, mathematics and single award science.

☛ **Articled Teachers' Scheme** started in September 1990. Articled teachers are graduates and are school based, spending two years training for the Postgraduate Certificate of Education.

☛ **Licensed Teachers' Scheme:** entrants must be over 26, hold GCSEs at grades A, B or C in English, mathematics and single award science, and have undertaken a higher education course lasting two years full-time or the equivalent part-time (eg DipHE, BTEC HND/HNC) for the two-year school-based training.

Teaching disabled children

For teaching deaf, blind, physically or mentally disabled children the ordinary course (see above) should be taken. An additional course in teaching disabled children is taken after gaining some teaching experience. It is necessary before teaching blind or deaf children and recommended before teaching other disabled children.

✍ **Further information** Teaching as a Career (TASC), Department for Education, Sanctuary Buildings, Great Smith Street, Westminster, London SW1P 3BT

▥ **Reading** *A Career in Teaching* published by and available free from the Department for Education
The NATFHE Handbook of Initial Teacher Training copies of which can be found in most libraries and careers offices
☛ School careers library classification FAB

Textile technology

Textile technologists apply their scientific knowledge to the manufacture and use of fibre, yarns and fabrics for the production of clothing, furnishings and carpets (see also Dyeing).

☛ Full-time or part-time college courses for a BTEC
National Certificate/Diploma in Textiles. Four GCSEs at
grades A, B or C or a BTEC First Certificate/Diploma are
required. The BTEC National awards can be followed by
study for the BTEC Higher National Certificate/Diploma
in Textiles and study for the Textile Institute's
examinations. The BTEC Higher award courses can also
be entered after sixth-form study. Three GCSEs at grades
A, B or C, including mathematics, a physical science and a
subject testing the use of English, and one A-level are
required.

☛ Full-time or part-time study for the Textile Institute's
Associateship examinations at recognised centres. Five
GCSEs at grades A, B or C, including mathematics and
two science subjects, together with one A-level in any
subject are required. All GCSE subjects are acceptable.

☛ Three- to four-year degree course in textiles or in a
relevant subject such as chemistry, and a one-year
postgraduate diploma. A good base of GCSEs at grades A,
B or C and at least two A-levels are required. For courses
in textile design or textile management the A-levels can be
in any subject; GCSEs in art, mathematics, physics and
chemistry are preferred. For courses in textile chemistry,
A-levels in chemistry and physics are required and A-level
mathematics is preferred. See GCSEs and higher
education on page 132.

✍ **Further information** The Textile Institute,
10 Blackfriars Street, Manchester M3 5DR

☛ School careers library classification SAG

Tourism
see **Travel and tourism work**

Town planning

Most planners work for local authorities drawing up
broad plans for development, allocating areas for

residential use, industrial use and open space. All future development and redevelopment must accord with these plans. Developers submit planning applications and planning permission is either granted or refused. Increasing numbers of planners are employed in the private sector.

Professional planners

☞ Four-year full-time, five-year sandwich or six-year part-time undergraduate courses for a degree or diploma in planning, giving exemption from the Final Examination of the Royal Town Planning Institute. At least three GCSEs, including English, mathematics and either history, geography or a language other than English, and two A-levels are recommended. Some colleges require A-level mathematics and some require a science, geography or economics.
☞ Degree in any subject, although degrees in related subjects such as economics, geography or law are sometimes preferred, followed by a two-year full-time or three-year part-time postgraduate course. See GCSEs and higher education on page 132.

Planning technicians

☞ Part-time or full-time college course for a BTEC Certificate/Diploma in Land Use. Four GCSEs at grades A, B or C, including mathematics and a subject testing use of English, or a BTEC First Certificate/Diploma are required for entry. This can be followed by BTEC Higher National Certificates/Diplomas. These courses can also be entered after sixth-form study; four GCSEs at grades A, B or C, including English and mathematics, and one A-level are required for entry. Holders of these Higher awards can become Members of the Society of Town Planning Technicians, provided they also have four years' practical experience.
✍ **Further information** The Royal Town Planning Institute, 26 Portland Place, London W1N 4BE
The Society of Town Planning Technicians, at the same address

📖 **Reading** *Careers in Town Planning* and *General Information about Membership* published by and available free from the Royal Town Planning Institute
A Career as a Town Planning Technician for School Leavers published by and available from the Society of Town Planning Technicians
☛ School careers library classification US

Trading standards administration

Trading standards officers (sometimes called consumer protection officers) enforce the wide range of legislation promoting and protecting fair and safe trading practices, such as the Trade Descriptions Act, the Weights and Measures Act and the Consumer Protection Act. They also advise and help members of the public, traders and business executives on trading issues, and in some areas also get involved in a much wider range of duties, such as consumer education and enforcing animal health laws.

☛ Three-year block-release course for the Diploma in Trading Standards while working for a local authority. Three GCSEs at grades A, B or C and two A-levels are required, including English, mathematics and physics at either level. Some of the candidates are graduates in any subject.

☛ Consumer advice officers take the Diploma in Consumer Affairs for which five GCSEs at grades A, B or C are required, including English.

✍ **Further information** The Institute of Trading Standards Administration, Suite 18, Thamesgate House, 37 Victoria Avenue, Southend-on-Sea SS2 6BU
Local Government Management Board, Arndale House, Arndale Centre, Luton LU1 2TS

📖 **Reading** *A Career as a Trading Standards Officer* published by and available free from the Institute of Trading Standards Administration

☛ School careers library classification COP

Traffic warden

Traffic wardens work under the direction of the police to ensure a smooth flow of traffic. They check that parking regulations are complied with and head school crossing patrols.

☛ On-the-job training in traffic warden work. There are no formal entry qualifications. Minimum age is 18; successful candidates are usually older than 18.

✍ **Further information** Local Chief Constable – the address will be in the local telephone directory

☛ School careers library classification MAB

Travel and tourism work

Travel agents arrange holidays and business travel for the public. They sell air, coach and train tickets, make hotel bookings and sell holidays arranged by the tour operators. Tour operators organise complete holidays at competitive prices.

☛ The ABTA NTB Youth Training (YT) Programme is for 16/17 year-olds. The programme will help you to achieve the Certificate in Travel Skills and the Diploma in Travel Skills. These are National Vocational Qualifications at Levels 2 and 3. As well as these Retail Travel qualifications there are also openings and qualifications available in business travel, tour operating and airlines. You can only join the Programme as a trainee employed in the travel industry. There are no formal entry requirements, but successful applicants often have three or four GCSEs at grades A, B or C. Selection concentrates on the appearance, enthusiasm, personality and common sense of the candidate. A flexible approach to work is also important.

☛ Full-time or part-time college courses for a BTEC National Certificate/Diploma in Business and Finance (Travel and Tourism). Four GCSEs at grades A, B or C or a BTEC First award with credit are required for entry. There are no formal entry requirements for the BTEC First award. The BTEC National awards can be followed by study for the BTEC Higher National Certificate/ Diploma in Business and Finance with travel and tourism options. These courses can also be entered with three GCSEs at grades A, B or C and one A-level. Holders of the BTEC Higher National Diploma in Business and Finance with appropriate options gained at a college approved by the Institute are eligible to become full members of the Institute of Travel and Tourism.

☛ Degree course in tourism at some universities and colleges of higher education. It is also possible to take a degree in any subject and follow it with a postgraduate course in tourism.

✍ **Further information** The Institute of Travel and Tourism, 113 Victoria Street, St Albans, Hertfordshire AL1 3TJ (please send a stamped addressed envelope and £3.00 to cover costs)

Association of British Travel Agents National Training Board (ABTA NTB), Waterloo House, 11–17 Chertsey Road, Woking, Surrey GU21 5AL (a large stamped addressed envelope must be enclosed)

▥ **Reading** *Working In* series: *Tourism* published by and available from the Careers and Occupational Information Centre, price £2.95

The Handbook of Tourism and Leisure published by Hobsons Publishing PLC, price £6.50

☛ School careers library classification GAX

Typography
see **Printing**

aluation

see **Estate agency, auctioneering and valuation**

Veterinary nursing

Veterinary nurses, formerly called animal nursing auxiliaries, help veterinary surgeons treat animal illnesses and accidents.

☛ Four GCSEs at grades A, B or C, including English and a single award science (preferably double award science) or mathematics, are required for enrolment as a trainee under a scheme administered by the Royal College of Veterinary Surgeons. All subjects are acceptable. Minimum age is 17. Two years' full-time gainful employment in an approved veterinary practice or centre and successful completion of preliminary and final examinations are required for admission to the List of Veterinary Nurses. Full-time courses may be attended for up to six months of the two-year training period. It is not possible for a veterinary nurse to become a veterinary surgeon.

✍ **Further information** The British Veterinary Nursing Association, The Seedbed Centre, Coldharbour Road, Harlow, Essex CM19 5AF

▥ **Reading** Free leaflet and Guide to the Scheme published by the Association, price £4.00 including postage

Working In series: *Animals – Work With* published by and available from the Careers and Occupational Information Centre, price £2.65

☛ School careers library classification WAL

Veterinary work

Veterinary surgeons, commonly known as 'vets', treat sick and injured animals. In the towns the animals would be household pets, while a country vet treats mainly farm animals.

☛ Five- or six-year degree course in veterinary science. A good base of GCSEs at grades A, B or C, including mathematics and double award science, and three A-levels are required for entry. Generally the A-level requirements are biology, zoology, chemistry and either physics or mathematics.

✍ **Further information** Royal College of Veterinary Surgeons, 32 Belgrave Square, London SW1X 8QP

▥ **Reading** A free leaflet and *A Career as a Veterinary Surgeon* published by the Royal College of Veterinary Surgeons, price £4.00 post free

Veterinary Science Degree Course Guide published by Hobsons Publishing PLC, price £4.99

☞ School careers library classification WAL

Weights and measures inspection
see **Trading standards administration**

Wholesaling
see **Retail and wholesale distribution**

Word processing
see **Secretarial work**

Youth and community work

Youth workers help young people to run clubs and other youth organisations. Community workers do similar work for people of all ages and take on the role of organiser, counsellor and welfare officer at a community centre.

☞ Two-year full-time Diploma in Higher Education (DipHE) course for youth workers and/or community centre wardens. Five GCSEs at grades A, B or C will normally be required. Minimum age is generally 23.

☛ A good base of GCSEs at grades A, B or C and at least two A-levels are required for a degree in any subject followed by a one-year full-time postgraduate training course.

✍ **Further information** National Youth Agency, 17–23 Albion Street, Leicester LE1 6GD

▥ **Reading** *Initial Training Courses in Youth and Community Work* published by and available from the National Youth Agency, price £3.95

☛ School careers library classification KEG

Zookeeping

Zookeepers care for animals in zoos and safari parks. See also Veterinary nursing.

☛ On-the-job training for animal keepers together with a correspondence course (National Extension College) for City and Guilds examinations. Formal educational qualifications are not usually essential, but preference is often given to candidates with some GCSEs at grade E or above in biological subjects, English and mathematics.

☛ A degree in zoology. A good base of GCSEs at grades A, B or C and at least two A-levels in biology, chemistry and either physics or mathematics are generally required, and if these subjects are not held at A-level they should be held at GCSE. See GCSEs and higher education on page 132. There are limited opportunities for professional zoologists in zoos, but other posts are open to them.

✍ **Further information** Zoological Society of London, Regent's Park, London NW1 4RY and local zoos

▥ **Reading** *Careers in Zoology* and *Zookeeping* both published by and available from the Zoological Society of London

Working In series: *Animals – Work With* published by and available from the Careers and Occupational Information Centre, price £2.65

☛ School careers library classification WAM